LIVING MYTHS

LIVING MYTHS

How Myth Gives Meaning to Human Experience

J. F. BIERLEIN

BALLANTINE WELLSPRING™
THE BALLANTINE PUBLISHING GROUP
NEW YORK

A Ballantine Wellspring™ Book
Published by The Ballantine Publishing Group

http://www.randomhouse.com/BB/

Library of Congress Cataloging-in-Publication Data
Bierlein, J. F.
    Living myths : how myth gives meaning to human experience /
J. F. Bierlein.—1st ed.
       p.   cm.
    Includes bibliographical references.
    ISBN 0-345-42207-4 (pbk. : alk. paper)
    1. Mythology.   I. Title.
  BL311.B535   1999
  291.1'3—dc21   98-38533
                                                  CIP

Cover illustration by Larry Schwinger

Manufactured in the United States of America

First Edition: April 1999

10 9 8 7 6 5 4 3 2 1

To Heather

Contents

Acknowledgments

I would like to thank the following people for their encouragement, interest, and friendship during the writing of this book:

My wife, Heather Diehl, to whom this book is dedicated;

My family (John, Germaine, John Fowler, Cheryl, Elisabeth, Susan, John B. III, Martha, and Sara) and in-laws (Bob, Jane, Atala, Rick, Mid, and Bill);

My editors at Ballantine Books, Elizabeth Zack, Lewis Robinson, and Jason Zuzga;

My Northwood University colleagues, Robert Serum and Grover Proctor;

My CSR friend and colleague, Pat Maher;

My American University colleagues, Richard Semiatin, Dave Brown, Brent Griffith, Seth Heim, Kay King, Donna Chapman, and others;

My godchildren, Marco Clavel and Liz Holder;

Many friends, including Gerard and Martha Holder, Father Roberto Morales, Irma Morales, John and Deb Selby, Mike Kenney, Steve Johnson, Dan Gallagher, Kate Rudebeck, and Don and Wendi Mitchell.

Author's Note

This book is the product of a series of questions that have been posed to me by people since the publication of the first of my books on myth, *Parallel Myths*, in 1994. The earlier work looked at themes in mythology, theories of interpretation, and the similarities between myths of different cultures. This book is the result of the logical next step in our inquiry into myth and its meaning: How does myth provide meaning to human existence? It looks to the truths of human experience that were reflected in the lives of people centuries ago, and the relevance of those truths today.

In order to examine the role of myth in finding meaning, it was necessary to divide human existence into experiences that we all know. The first chapter is on fathers and sons. While one on mothers and daughters would be useful, the traditional myths are generally fairly patriarchal. Luckily some of the same issues can be applied across gender. The next chapter, which deals with myths of romantic love, develops the complex images and meanings of men and women in their lives together; in this chapter the strength of women is manifest throughout. There is much that can be done to develop these two topics further, but my goal here is to provide the reader with a map for further investigation.

In the subsequent chapters the myths of nature and human nature speak to our place in the cosmos. There are myths of the hero that speak to our individual struggle for our existence. And the foundation myths are about the collective identities of peoples and nations, providing a matrix for their histories.

One omission is that of death and the afterlife. Because of the complexity of the subject and the number of myths that focus on this mystery, the topic requires its own rather lengthy book—one I have yet to write! The chapter on nature and human nature does touch briefly on the issue to provoke greater thinking and inspire further investigation.

Taken together, the myths contained within reflect humankind's, and our, search for meaning in human existence. *Living Myths* offers a record of that search, and the answers that speak to us today. The myths constitute, as the conclusion is entitled, an "Eternal Mirror" in which we see all humanity as well as our own faces.

J. F. BIERLEIN
Falls Church, Virginia, 1998

Introduction
Myth and Meaning

Faith can mean nothing else but the conviction that life as such, with all its mysteries, all its horrors, and all its marvels, has a meaning.

—Arthur Schnitzler, Austrian playwright (1862–1931)

The world in which we are born is brutal and cruel, and at the same time a thing of divine beauty. Which element we think outweighs the other, whether meaninglessness or meaning, is a matter of temperament. If meaninglessness were absolutely preponderant, the meaningfulness of life would vanish to an increasing degree with each step in our development. Probably, as in all metaphysical questions, both are true. Life is—or has—meaning and meaninglessness. I cherish the anxious hope that meaning will preponderate and win the battle.

—Carl G. Jung, Swiss psychoanalyst (1875–1961)

Does life have meaning? This book is about not only the meaning of the myths, but the more important matter of how myth gives meaning to human existence.

Meaning. There are days when life appears to be merely a

crazy quilt, a random collection of episodes, punctuated by inevitable failures, victories great and small, moments of joy, grief, and loss, and simple absurdity. Yet, when life is viewed as a totality, a continuous process of growth, each event has meaning as part of something greater than itself. In the myths, we see attempts to comprehend the cosmos, and the roles, however small, we as humans play. We see ourselves as part of the totality of the cosmos. We see patterns of growth and recovery in the face of life's starker realities. Myth shows the way others have worked at reconciling the opposing forces at work in human experience.

Collectively, as nations, we seek meaning and create sacred civic histories. Being an American, a Canadian, or a Swiss is more than being born on a given side of a river. Nationality and nationhood are complex matrices of beliefs, symbols, "magic" words, that provide us individually and collectively with identity, the meaning of our nation, and the mythic dimensions of its past that direct our future. Nationality is based on civic myths that we live in daily, consciously or not.

The great problem of human life always has been and still is that of finding a meaning or purpose, an aim toward which one may direct one's efforts. In the disciplines of theology, philosophy, psychiatry, and literature, the meaning of life has always been the central question. The sharpness and urgency of this question seem to have increased throughout the twentieth century and still follow us into the new century.

The challenges to human existence, both as individuals and as societies, seem greater than ever. My own generation, the eighty million Americans and nearly ten million Canadians born in the 1950s and 1960s, are now at a point in their lives where the question of meaning seems urgent and elusive in an environment of social polarization, gratuitous violence, and a quest for perceived lost "family values." Religion was and is a compass through that existence, and our myths have been the road map of meaning. We may doubt the existence of higher realities, but we ache to see them at work in our world. That breakthrough of something beyond objective reality into our objective world is the *numinous*—from the Latin word *numen*, or supernatural being. A sacred history, common to all mythic systems, is a record of the numinous in the human past that is both a pattern for the present, and in the words of German philosopher Martin Heidegger (1889–1976), the "eternal now" that is always there, but only truly real as we encounter it.

A useful way to understand how myth speaks to us is to keep in mind the six critical elements of the human condition as set out by contemporary French existentialist philosopher Paul Ricoeur (born 1913): Ricoeur proposed that, in order for humans to be at peace with their lives, they need to address these six issues in their lives: (1) our *finitude*; (2) our *estrangement* from God and/or the numinous; (3) our process of *becoming and transcendence*, in that in each human life, the truth is never whole and complete; (4) the paradox of *the freedom and burden of human choice*; (5) our *existence with, in, and through others*, for our sense of meaning is relational; and ultimately, (6) our *identity and participation* in the cosmos.

By *finitude*, we mean the realization that there are limits to our "sight" (our understanding and our reasoning), and that life, too, is limited. We can never apprehend the numinous in a complete form, and the process of "revelation" and the language of mythology are efforts to understand the reality of God, or the numinous, acting in human history and experience in terms accessible to and understood by human beings.

We are also finite in that we know the inevitability of our own death and the anxiety that this causes. As the German writer Hermann Hesse (1877–1962) bluntly put it:

> *Das Leben ist doch so beschissen*
> *Weil wir alle sterben müssen*

> Life is certainly shitty since everybody must die.

The issue of human finitude gives an urgency to the sense of meaning. Not only do the myths speak to the possibilities, meaning, and realities of a worthwhile life, they also concern themselves with what happens when we die.

The issue of *estrangement* permeates the myths. Invariably, many myths tell of a "time before time" wherein God (or the gods) and humans lived in a companionable fellowship that was broken through sin or perhaps an action on the part of the Creator to absent himself or herself from the creation; this belief is common to virtually all cultures. Estrangement pervades two modes of our thinking: our subjective selves and our faculty of feeling, which yearn for something beyond ourselves and ache to see God or the numinous active in the world, and our objective reasoning, which seems to rule out the possibility of the supernatural acting directly in human history, and in our personal histories as well.

The process of reconciliation and renewed fellowship is a key theme throughout the myths. What can transcend this estrangement? This is a central question in the myths of the past and our own today.

> Man is part of nature, subject to her physical laws and unable to change them, yet he transcends the rest of nature. He is set apart while being a part; he is homeless yet chained to the home he shares with all creatures. Cast

into this world at an accidental place and time, he is forced out of it, again, accidentally. Being aware of himself, he realizes his powerlessness and the limitations of his existence.

—Erich Fromm, German American psychoanalyst (1900–1980)

Limited in his nature, infinite in his desires, man is a fallen god who remembers the heavens.

—Alphonse de Lamartine, French poet (1790–1869)

The process of *becoming and transcendence* is yet another consistent theme in the myths and is a source of hope for us all. The hero might be born to his quest, but although born to be a hero, he also has to *become* a hero. The hero goes through trials and is never entirely invincible; he must transcend defeats. Here is an entry point, for like any of us, the hero loses sometimes. And yet, the hero becomes a hero through the realization of his quest; in the same manner, we all become ourselves through the realization of work and the search for truth. As American mythologist Joseph Campbell (1904–1987) wrote, "The hero is every man." In the trials and transcendence offered in the myths of the heroes, we see ourselves and we see meaning. And so it is in every life: we are always in the process of becoming whom we are.

Each new life situation demands something new of us that causes us to change in ways both small and great. Thus the hero of the myths is always faced with the paradox of the *freedom and burden of* critical *choices*, both in the context of ethical ambiguity and in terms of the risks inherent in every choice. In the Christian and Jewish traditions, it was through the exercise of free will—choice—that sin, and thus estrangement, took place. In Greek mythology, estrangement from the

gods took place when Prometheus stole fire from heaven and
Pandora opened the box whence the ills of the world sprang;
these were acts of human choice. For us, it means asking the
question, *Do I make my choices or do my choices make me?*
Here is truth as paradox, for both are true.

In our own lives and the lives of the heroes, there is always
the certainty of tragedy and the anguished hope of transcendence that gives meaning to human experience. The myths
provide models of transcendence that help us find a means
to transcend difficulties and sorrows and invest life with
meaning.

> Life is an operation which is done in a forward direction.
> One lives toward the future, because to live consists inex-
> orably in doing, in each individual life making itself.
>
> —José Ortega y Gasset, Spanish philosopher (1883–1955)

The myths remind us as well that our *existence*, and its
meaning, are *with, in, and through others*. Our process of
becoming cannot take place in isolation. Children receive an
identity from their parents, yet strive to establish their own
individuality. The myths speak to the power of love to transform both the lover and the beloved; this love gives meaning
to life. The hero cannot become a hero alone, and the heroic
myths include mentors, friends, lovers, allies, and, above all,
enemies who define the hero. Each of these relationships is
necessary for the hero to take up his quest.

Myths can act to invest our lives—our existence—with
meaning. They give us our *identity* in the cosmos, a perspective of our place in the entirety of things. Our identities as citi-
zens, children, lovers, workers, and the minor-league heroes
we are in our own houses are reflected in the myths of many

cultures and times. Inasmuch as we seek to find how myths have given meaning to people throughout history, we should also consider the myths as meditations on events that touch every life and affirm the value of life in the face of its realities.

One day when I was home sick with the flu, I noticed how, viewed close up, there appeared to be no order to the quilt that my mother had made; for years I had appreciated its neat pattern from the perspective of the whole. The little patches in the quilt had their value only as part of the overall pattern. Thus, as the myths teach us, meaning is derived from taking the parts and seeing a whole. Seeing that one has a role in the cosmos automatically conveys a sense of purpose and place; this is what is affirmed in the myths.

The American playwright Eugene O'Neill (1888–1953) once wrote to his children that the secret of life was contained in a simple phrase: "Man is born broken; he lives by mending; and the grace of God is the glue." It is only by viewing life as a process, a collection of meanings bound together by a thread, that life can offer the joy that is found in a sense of meaning. The myths are threads for the process of mending. The threads may fray and break, but we know that there is a pattern being sewn.

In the life of every individual human being, the process of finding a meaning, embracing that sense of meaning totally, and living a worthwhile life often appears to be a hit-or-miss proposition. The realities of growing older, of parenthood, losing our loved ones, economic displacement, and the sense of brevity of our own lives often make us question the meaning of our existence, and certainly that of happiness.

Few topics have received such agonized attention as the search for meaning, especially in the first half of the twentieth century. The decline of a religious worldview and the shattering of old civic myths—following the destruction of the stable order people had known before World War I—created anxiety and urgency. The two fruits of this inquisitive process were both existential philosophy and a renewed interest in the value of myth. Religion, myth, and any book with the word *soul* in the title have become hot commodities today. Why?

For roughly the past 150 years, it has been widely believed that science and technology alone might eventually solve all human problems, that progress is inevitable, and that history moves in a linear direction toward a technological utopia. (If you doubt this, go back and look at films of Disney's Tomorrowland from the early sixties or watch old newsreels of the 1939 and 1964 New York World Fairs. The record of technological and scientific progress is stunning, and this progress has been extraordinary in extending, improving, and safeguarding human life. The world in which my grandmother was born was a world of horses and buggies, the telephone, and Victrolas—with an average human life expectancy of under fifty years. The world in which she died was the world of cloning, cyberlinkage, "designer" genetics in agriculture, and MTV—with an average human life expectancy of seventy-eight years.) The stage for the twentieth-century problem of meaning was set in the nineteenth. Throughout the past 150 years, a philosophical system called *positivism* held sway and precluded the possibility of accidents, the numinous, miracles, or randomness. Positivism held that the scientific method of investigation could be applied to the study of anything. As positivism grew in influence, the realms of feeling and intuition, the "unseen" worlds of God, and our subjective human impressions were diminished in influence or value and at times categorically negated. Science and myth were set against each other as enemies.

Yet the scientific mode of thinking, in itself, has not been able to provide human beings with a sense of meaning. In fact, rational scientific thinking perceived the traditional sources of meaning—namely myth, religion, and philosophical speculation—as outmoded. Given this increase in objectivity, there has been a diminishing sense of that most subjective thing—meaning—in human life.

Not only has science not been able to answer the question of meaning, it has raised new questions of meaning! Many of us support capital punishment but fight such practices as euthanasia and abortion. We are able to prolong the quantity of life through medical advances, but this provokes anguished debates over the quality of life.

We would do well to remember that science and religion can answer two very different questions. Science tells us *how* things happen, by identifying the causes of things as can be observed, identified, and described by our five senses (empirically) or quantitatively through precise measurements, mathematical, or statistical analyses. Science is objective and studies objects. Religion and myth answer *why* things happen—not in terms of causes, but in terms of purpose and meaning, a subjective understanding.

The difference between causative "how" thinking (scientific) and purposive "why" thinking (religious) can be illustrated using the analogy of a wristwatch. You may take a wristwatch apart—tiny spring by tiny spring—and if you are attentive, you will see "how" the watch works, by identifying what gear causes which hand to move. However, as useful as this information might be, it tells you nothing of the purpose of the watch, let alone why we need to tell time. It does not explain the anxiety we feel about keeping appointments. And it offers no consolation when the boss chides us for not being on time.

In our inquiry as to the difference between these two modes of thinking, it is important to think in terms of phenomenon and noumenon. A phenomenon is something that can be perceived empirically. The noumenon, in contrast, is something that can be known only through intellectual intuition, experience, or feeling; it is something felt, apprehended, or grasped. The word *phenomenon* comes from the Greek verbs *phainesthai* (to appear) and *phanein* (to show). *Noumenon*, on the other hand, comes from a very different source. It comes from *nous*, the word used by both Plato and Aristotle to signify *mind*. It is also a first cousin to *gnosis*, or knowledge.

Think about the distinction between *knowing a person* and *knowing a fact*. Knowing a person has a qualitative, subjective quality: I know my friend is kind, intelligent, funny, a bit self-indulgent, but warmhearted. But knowing that two and two make four is a very different kind of knowledge.

Interestingly, the greatest assault on the objectivity of science came from a scientist. German physicist Werner Heisenberg (1901–1976) was a rare man, winning the 1932 Nobel Prize for his work in quantum mechanics and devoting himself to philosophical speculations in his later life. Heisenberg wrote a paper in 1927 that established the Heisenberg indeterminacy principle. What Heisenberg said was that scientific inquiry *is never and cannot be entirely objective*. All observations are colored by the subjectivity of the investigator. Even in strictly quantitative endeavors, the observer undertakes a qualitative allocation of value to what is seen.

On that basis, the causative and purposive blur together. And in our reading of the myths, *the causative and the purposive are thoroughly blended together*. The myth of Kore, for instance, tells us about the origins of spring—nature—on one level and discusses the question of life after death—human nature—on another. The story of Isis and Osiris tells us why the Nile rises when it does, and also discusses life after death.

The question of meaning has always been answered in terms of knowing whom we are and why we are here. It is the numinous—the appearance in objective reality of something beyond that reality—that gives us a sense of meaning and always has. Moses doesn't lead his people out of the desert simply because Egypt is unpleasant. Rather, the numinous appearance of the burning bush, the plagues against Egypt, and the parting of the Red Sea all give a numinous and living meaning to the Exodus. Passover is a retelling and reliving of that sacred history in the present. Our sacred history is a record of meanings that give meaning to human experience in the present, not merely a linear list of dates; the same can be said of civic myths. And so, meaning starts with the apprehension of a Great Mystery in which we take part. And investing life with meaning *is where myth begins to function.*

Thus, our inquiry in *Living Myths* is to see how myths are a road map of the human experience common to us all, and that they speak clearly to who we are as finite creatures, estranged from the numinous, living out a process of becoming and transcendence, making choices, living in societies and families, and finding our identity and place in the cosmos. This road map and our sense of our place in the cosmos begins with our most elemental human experiences: as parents and children.

1. Fathers and Sons

There is no more basic human experience than that of parent and child. The myths that follow concern perennial issues between fathers and sons. In doing so, they convey lessons about behavior and human nature. In later chapters, we will see mothers and daughters, mothers and sons, and fathers and daughters interacting in the myths. Here, too, the interactions are eternal; only the specifics are different.

In some of the myths that follow, we see a father contemplating killing his own son to please the gods, showing that there are limits to the transactions that can be conducted between gods and men. Clearly, in these myths it is the gods who have the upper hand—yet the gods ultimately affirm the value of human life.

In the latter myths in this chapter, we see moral parables contrasting the braggadocio of youth with the mellowness and wisdom of age. In all three tales a youth talks himself into a difficult situation. Clearly these myths expose both the results of swaggering machismo and the certain competitive element that always exists between fathers and sons.

And the myth of Phaëthon is a powerful story of love versus

indulgence in a parental relationship. The father, who loves his son, promises him anything within his power; the son asks the one thing the father will not grant.

Beyond the apparent morals offered in these myths, the myths also offer insights into specific cultures. One can see how the Greeks and Romans, the people of Israel, the Norse, and the Algonquins saw themselves both in society and in the parent-child relationship. What Thor brags about and how Odin responds tell us about the male values in Norse culture; the lesson of the Algonquin story of Grandfather, Father, and Son speaks to the issue of the individual versus the community. Ultimately, all of these stories offer culturally specific and universal insights. The roles of women in these myths, or the paucity thereof, have something important to say as well. In the patriarchal societies that predominate in this chapter, men are the focus not only of intergenerational conflict, but of the struggle between fathers and sons for identity, power, and legitimacy. The paucity of women in these stories may, as we will see, be a record of a "history of prehistory," reflecting the distant memory of the battle between a patriarchy and an earlier matriarchal society.

In returning to the six elements of human existence, age readily accepts the *finitude* of our lives—a lesson that youth can only learn painfully. In the first two stories, sacrifices are offered to bridge the sense of *estrangement* from the gods, only for the gods to impose limits. The stories of Athamas and Phrixus, Abraham and Isaac, and the Algonquin story of Grandfather, Father, and Son all point to *transcending* truths learned at a cost. The stories of fathers and sons are stories also of *becoming* fathers and sons in a dynamic relationship that constantly redefines itself through *interaction*. All of these stories illustrate the *freedom and burden* of human choice, for which a price must be paid. And, much as myths define our identity in the cosmos, we both receive an *identity* from our fathers and rebel against them to establish individual identities.

ATHAMAS AND PHRIXUS
(Greece)

This story is a prologue to the well-known adventure of Jason and the Argonauts. It is notable in its similarity to the story of Abraham and Isaac and is believed to share the same original source—probably the Semitic people of Mesopotamia, or perhaps it was spread by the trading Phoenician neighbors of Israel. The tale of the youth wrongly accused, as given here, of adultery is a common ancient theme, found in the Bible story of Joseph and Potiphar's wife, and the Egyptian tale of the Two Brothers.

Athamas had a son named Phrixus. As the boy grew, he became very handsome, so much so that his aunt (by marriage) fell hopelessly in love with him. When Phrixus rejected her advances, telling her that it was wrong to sleep with his uncle's wife, she spread the rumor that it was Phrixus who had tried to seduce *her*. The word spread throughout the world until it reached the god Apollo, who was outraged at such immorality. Apollo decreed that Phrixus must die, and because a form of incest was involved (although Phrixus's aunt was not a blood relative), Athamas must carry out the execution of his own son.

Athamas wept as he took Phrixus to the mountaintop; his hands shook as he took the knife to slit his son's throat. Just as Athamas was ready to strike the fatal blow, the hero Heracles

(Roman: Hercules) appeared and bellowed, "My father Zeus is revolted by human sacrifice!" Zeus (Roman: Jupiter), who knew that Phrixus was innocent, sent at that moment a golden ram to the mountaintop. Phrixus climbed on its back and off they flew to safety.

Zeus's wife Hera (Roman: Juno), enraged that Athamas would believe his sister-in-law's lies, struck Athamas absolutely mad to the point that he lived like an animal, eating grass.

As for the golden ram, its fleece became the Golden Fleece that was later sought by Jason and the Argonauts.

Connections

The myth of Athamas and Phrixus speaks to the existential element of estrangement from the gods, and Greek gods who strongly resemble humans.

In this story, humans are so alienated from the gods that a wrongful judgment is rendered by the god Apollo, who readily accepts the false witness of Phrixus's aunt and sentences the lad to death without bothering to consider Phrixus's account. One condition of youth has always been their elders' unwillingness to accept their credibility.

The Greek gods, in this myth and others, are mirrors of ourselves. They disagree and act rashly, even unfairly. Apollo, too, is finite in his sight. Yet the story of Athamas and Phrixus affirms the principle of divine justice, as Zeus intervenes, not only to stop an unjust execution, but also to assert the value of human life through abhorrence of human sacrifice.

With respect to the relationship between fathers and sons, it is important to remember that Zeus had to intervene because Athamas readily believed the false charges against his son and was prepared to carry out the sentence of death pronounced by Apollo. Athamas did not believe Phrixus's side of the story and did little to help. Athamas's pleas and anguish were based on love of his son—not on faith that his own son was telling the truth. Fathers, in cases both great and small, may love their sons, but often make judgments about them whether fair or not. One also has to wonder whether Athamas experienced some element of jealousy over his son's handsomeness and youth. But ultimately, the story is an assertion that divine justice is superior to filial piety, and the gods demand that even a father must pay for misjudging his own son. A father may be master in his own house, but even that father must answer to a master.

The fact that the golden ram is sent by Zeus at just the right moment and that its fleece later becomes the hard-won prize sought by Jason and the Argonauts speaks to the issue of human estrangement. The Golden Fleece is a token of the numinous, evidence that Zeus (and thus divine justice) intervened in human history. Much as the medieval heroes sought the Holy Grail (the chalice used by Christ in the Last Supper Seder) and invested it with great supernatural power, so did the Argonauts risk their lives to find the Golden Fleece as they invested it with power. Human beings inherently quest for "proofs" of the numinous, and hunger to overcome their estrangement from it.

ABRAHAM AND ISAAC
(The Bible and Talmud)

This story, which appears in Genesis 21 and 22, has long been both an admonition to faith, a statement on Israel's covenant with God, and a paradox that bears an important existential truth. One interesting note: in the Islamic version of the story, it is Ismail, ancestor of the Arabs, and not Isaac, who is brought to the sacrifice.

The patriarch Abram had two sons by two different mothers. The elder son, Ishmael (or Ismail, in Arabic), was the son of Abram by his Egyptian handmaiden, Hagar. The younger son was the result of a miracle.

The old patriarch Abram had reached his nineties and his beloved wife, Sarai, the age of eighty-nine. For decades the couple had accepted her barrenness. So Sarai had agreed for Abram to have a child by Hagar, his Egyptian handmaiden, as she knew that he must have an heir. Thus, Ishmael was born. Ishmael was the ancestor of the Arabs (and Muslims count him as a direct ancestor of the prophet Muhammad).

But God had other plans. When Abram turned ninety-nine years old, God changed his name from Abram to Abraham, meaning *father of many nations*, and renamed Sarai, Sarah, meaning *princess*. Abraham at first took this as a cruel joke and asked God how he and Sarah could have a child at such an advanced age. God replied that it was His will that Abraham be the father of many nations and announced that the ninety-year-old Sarah would conceive and bear a child within the year.

Not long after, three strangers appeared at Abraham's tent. While Abraham was out selecting a calf to feed them, one of the strangers pointed at a tent and said, "Next year, Sarah will give birth to a child in that tent." Sarah overheard them and burst into laughter. The strangers confronted Sarah about her laughter, which she then denied.

Some months later Sarah delivered a boy, named him Isaac, and circumcised him on the eighth day in token of God's covenant with Abraham. And as his half brother, Ishmael, was ancestor of the Arabs, Isaac was the ancestor of the Jews and Philistines.

One day God spoke to Abraham at Beersheba and commanded the old patriarch to take his son and climb to Mount Moriah. Abraham responded that he had two sons; whom was he to bring? God then said, "Take the son you love best." Abraham responded that he loved both of his sons. God knew that Abraham preferred Isaac, and so said once more, "Take the son you love best."

Considering that Isaac was a miracle and the son of old age, Abraham did indeed love Isaac best and tended to ignore Ishmael. So he determined to take Isaac.

Mount Moriah was the mountain of sacrifice, so Abraham knew what God appeared to be asking, but kept it to himself. Abraham gathered some wood to build a sacrificial fire and brought out a donkey to carry the load. Then Abraham, Isaac, and two servants set out northward for Mount Moriah. Abraham then bade the servants to remain behind as he, Isaac, and the donkey proceeded up the mountain.

The Talmud tells us that as Abraham and Isaac were scaling the mountain, the fallen angel Samael, in the guise of an old man, whispered into Abraham's ear, "Do you really think that a loving, compassionate God would have you kill the son for whom you've waited a lifetime?" But Abraham ignored the tempter.

Undaunted, Samael appeared to Isaac and said, "That crazy father of yours wants to kill you!" Isaac also ignored the tempter.

Abraham and Isaac reached the summit, built an altar of stones, and placed the wood on the sacrificial altar. Then Isaac asked, "Father, where is the lamb for the sacrifice?" Abraham responded, "The Lord will provide one." The situation, though, became clear when Abraham began to tie Isaac with rope as one does to a lamb before the sacrifice. Nevertheless Isaac willingly cooperated and was placed on the altar. Just as Abraham took a knife in hand and prepared to deliver the fatal blow, God called out, "Abraham! Don't touch that boy! Since you were willing to sacrifice your own son, I know your heart is pure."

At that moment, God supplied a lamb that was caught in the brambles, and the father and son sacrificed it to God.

Connections

The familiar story of Abraham and Isaac is a problematic one. While it is traditionally construed to demonstrate how great Abraham's trust in God is, it makes God appear to be capricious, even cruel in imposing such a test. Isaac, the long-awaited son of Abraham and Sarah's old age, is also the son through whom God promised to bless the nations; certainly Abraham must have thought that Isaac would either be spared or replaced. Still, the story must be considered in the context of the ancient Semitic peoples.

The sacrifice of the firstborn son was relatively common among Abraham's neighbors and is referred to at many points throughout the Bible (2 Kings 23:10, 2 Chronicles 28:3 and 33:6). Apostates in Israel fell into the practice, particularly in devotion to Chemosh (2 Kings 3:27) and Moloch, which means *king* (2 Kings 23:10). Among the Semitic peoples, the sacrifice of a firstborn son was considered the ultimate expiation of sin (Micah 6:7). Remember as well in the Exodus narrative that the slaying of the firstborn sons of Egypt was the ultimate plague that moved Pharaoh to "let my people [Israel] go."

Both the story of Abraham and Isaac and that of Athamas

and Phrixus tell us that there are limits to the transactions between gods and humans. Moreover, these stories tell us of a different view of humankind: The gods of Greece and Israel abhor human sacrifice, and as people are in the image of the gods, so they have a peculiar value among all things in creation. This expression of humanism colors our worldview today. It gives a sense of what the covenant of Israel meant; the God of Israel was different from the gods of their neighbors, and Israel was a people apart.

This can be contrasted with ancient Mexico, where humankind was made by mixing blood with cornmeal. Therefore, the appropriate sacrifices back to the gods were human blood and cornmeal. In Babylonia and ancient Mexico, human beings were created to serve the gods; in Israel and Greece, they were created to provide the gods with fellowship.

Christians have often read the story of Abraham and Isaac as a prophetic prefiguration of God the Father sacrificing His son, Jesus Christ, on the wooden cross; medieval artists even drew upon the parallel between the wood to be used for the sacrifice of Isaac and the wood of the cross of Christ.

Truth and meaning are so often conveyed in the form of a paradox, especially in the realm of myth and religion, and this is true of the story of Abraham and Isaac. On the surface, it would appear that God is demanding the sacrifice of Isaac. But, more significantly, God is demanding that *Abraham give himself*, to the point of killing the one whom Abraham loves most: the long-awaited son Isaac. It is Abraham's complete giving of himself that makes the sacrifice of Isaac unnecessary.

The story also speaks powerfully to the existential elements of finitude, estrangement, and identity. Abraham recognizes his finitude, and as he believes that God sees beyond the limits of man's sight, so he is prepared to act by faith.

The story also speaks to the human sense of estrangement. Not only in ancient Israel, but throughout the myths of many cultures, death enters the world as humankind is estranged from God or the gods (in the Judeo-Christian and classical traditions, through sin). Thus, estrangement is perceived to be overcome only through death—whether our own (think of the Catholic term *beatific vision*, wherein the righteous see God "face-to-face" after death) or the sacrificial death of another, be it Isaac or Jesus. Abraham seeks to overcome estrangement by giving himself through the death of Isaac.

The Abraham and Isaac narrative speaks to the issue of identity as well, for Abraham and his descendants. Traditionally the Arabs and Jews count themselves as the descendants of Abraham.

In the Islamic version, it is Ismail, not Isaac, who is taken for the sacrifice. As noted in the introduction, the prophet Muhammad is counted as a direct descendant of Ismail, and some Muslim scholars consider this event an important point in Allah's revelation. To an Arab Muslim, this is his or her own sacred history.

The covenant relationship with God was the very definition of ancient Israel, and the definition still stands among Orthodox Jews. Jews are those who keep the covenant with God; this is both their sacred history and their identity. And, unlike their neighbors' gods, the God of Israel rejects the transaction of human sacrifice, instead asking for Israel's people to give themselves in obedience to the covenant, as codified in the Torah.

Abraham, as we have said, is asked by God not so much for the sacrifice of his own son as to give himself. This needs to be restated, as herein lies the father-son dynamic of the story. Abraham is defined by his son and is still spoken of as

Father Abraham even today. Abraham's identity is so dependent upon having an heir that even his name is changed to mean *father of nations*.

The son is a crucial element in who Abraham is, and the relationship with the son is the reflection of the relationship with God. Abraham waits ninety years for the birth of Isaac, a test of faith in God. As much as all fathers give a family identity to their sons, so, too, the father-son relationship is a "spiritual barometer" for the father, as what is most demanded of any father in the father-son relationship is the father's own self.

The paradoxes in this story bothered Danish philosopher Søren Kierkegaard (1813–1855) so much that he used it as the framework for a major philosophical investigation. The result was a classic of Christian existentialism: *Fear and Trembling*. For Kierkegaard, the story of Abraham and Isaac is a perfect place to begin an investigation of the limits of ethics, of the relationship between God and man, of the costs of faith, and ultimately of the meaning of our existence.

Through the story of Abraham, Kierkegaard addresses the problem of "the teleological suspension of the ethical." In other words, is the duty to God so great that one would act unethically in order to fulfill his will? Kierkegaard asks the question of whether it was ethical for Abraham to follow God's command and take Isaac to the place of sacrifice, without even telling Isaac's mother, Sarah, or the priest Eleazar. For Kierkegaard, using the example of Abraham, faith in God presented a paradox; it was not merely objective belief, but a subjective passion. Kierkegaard, and certainly modern people, would be appalled were their neighbor to take his or her son for sacrifice, claiming that God had commanded it so. Even if one reckons in the factor that sacrifice of the firstborn was a relatively common religious practice among Abraham's neighbors, it appears to be at once an act of supreme faith in God and an abomination. For Kierkegaard, faith in God has a price, and the passion cannot be understood unless experienced, "felt."

THOR AND ODIN
(Norse)

This story tells of the competitive confrontation of father and son in a truly Norse context of adventure, fighting, loving, and drinking. It is easy to imagine the story being told by the fire in a Viking lodge late on a winter night after the feasting.

Once as Thor, the god of thunder, was traveling around the earth, he reached a broad sea inlet that he could not cross in his vast stride. He looked to the other side and there saw an old man, whom he insolently called Harbard (hoar-beard or graybeard), who had a boat. He insolently demanded that the old man take him across. Thor did not recognize that the old man was his own father, Odin.

But Thor was so rude and disrespectful in his request that Odin decided to teach him a lesson. So at first, Odin simply ignored Thor. Then Thor called out, "Hey, old man, take me across. If you do so, I will share my food with you." Still, Odin would not respond.

Thor once more said, "Take me across. Don't you know who I am?" This time Odin responded. "I know who you are. You are disrespectful and a young drifter in search of adventure. I will not take you across."

Thor replied, "You evidently have no idea to whom you are

speaking." The thunder god began reciting his mighty deeds, telling stories of the giants he had slain. He finished by saying, "Old man, what were *you* doing when I was slaying giants?"

"Well," said Odin, "I was helping farmers grow crops. I was busy helping a king to ward off giants and enemies for five straight years. And then the king's daughter fell in love with me."

"How long ago was that?" sneered Thor. "And what king's daughter would ever *want* an old man like you?! You want to talk about women? I have had countless. Plus, I can outfight you and outdrink you any day. So, shut up and take me across the inlet!"

Odin responded sarcastically, "Oh, you have slain giants all right. I have heard stories of how you once cowered in fear before a giant and dressed up as a woman. I also know why you have to fight giants all the time: usually you end up fighting because you are stupid and blunder into situations that anyone with a brain would avoid. You end up fighting because you don't think. And, as for drinking, I have heard stories, as has everyone else, of how you have won great victories only to make a damned fool of yourself by drinking yourself blind drunk at the feasts afterward."

Thor's legendary anger began to burn. "Listen, don't talk back to me. Take me across the river or I'll . . ."

"You'll what?" replied Odin.

Thor spat out, "Forget about your boat, old man," and walked away.

About a week later, Thor realized that the boatman was his father. For quite a long time after, Thor was very sheepish around Odin.

Connections

This myth might be summarized as two things my mother always said: "It's nice to be important, but it is more important to be nice," and "Always be careful; you never know to whom you might be talking." Every culture has stories wherein one encounters a stranger who turns out to be something other than what he or she appears. For example, when Abraham favorably entertains three strangers at Mamre who turn out to be angels of the Lord, it causes him to accrue great favor in God's eyes.

This myth and the ones following it speak to the boldness of youth contrasted with the elements of age. In a more specific father-son context, they also speak to another truth-bearing paradox about the father and son relationship. We receive our basic identity from our fathers—a family name, and often our personal name (as those with *Junior, III*, etc., can attest)—and our fathers may even want us to be like them. We are to live up to, bring pride to, and build upon our family name. (A case to illustrate the connection between identity and fatherhood can be found in Russian culture, where the usual middle name is the patronymic; *Peter Ilyich Tchaikovsky*, translated, means *Peter, the son of Ilya [Elias], Tchaikovsky*.) The statement "He's just like his father," or "He's a chip off the old block," applied to a son is taken as a compliment that causes the father to beam; it usually annoys the son.

The paradox lies in that while the son is expected to proudly bear and live up to the father's family name, he is also expected to make a name for himself. Thus, the son is both given an identity from the father and must struggle to establish his own individual identity. Of course, this is an eternal theme in the struggle between fathers and sons.

In Russian writer Ivan Turgenev's (1818–1883) novel *Fathers and Sons*, this is, of course, the central theme. The father cannot believe that his son could be so different from him; the son cannot believe that this man could be *his* father. Yet the reader sees the father as a mirror image of the son; the two are very different, but have more character traits in common than either realizes.

A big part of the life of every young man is to differentiate himself from his father, to seek adventures to establish an authentic, independent identity. As any parent of an adolescent boy can tell you, these adventures can include reckless, rash, and bold exploits that the youth cannot dream the father would indulge in, let alone understand. However, when Dad's army buddy tells a few stories of Dad sowing wild oats, the son listens intently, yet incredulously.

In this myth, Odin knows that the young traveler is his son, but Thor does not recognize his own father in the ferryman. So Thor, with the characteristic rashness of youth, recites his bold exploits to impress this old man, but gets nowhere fast. Thor demands respect (without concerning himself about the matter of *earning* respect) by telling impressive tales of his own identity as Thor—as lover, fighter, drinker, and adventurer. Thor never tries to impress the ferryman by saying, "Don't you know who my father is?"—and this is no casual omission. Rather, this is the clear description of a young man struggling to create an impressive, individual identity.

But Thor does not recognize his own father. Even if Odin were *disguised* as a ferryman, one would think that Thor would at least recognize Odin's voice! In the next myth, Phaëthon knows his father, but obviously did not grow up with him, and seeks proof that Helios, his reputed father, is really his father.

Swiss scholar Johann Jakob Bachofen (1815–1887) and British poet-scholar Robert Graves (1895–1985) considered these myths as a record of both a distant matriarchal age and an intermediate battle between the sexes wherein women at first dominated the society and were later challenged; in such a society, boys either did not know their fathers or at least did not grow up with them.

Bachofen was fascinated by mythology and tried to sift through it to find a record of the earliest history of Europe. In reading the myths, Bachofen concluded that they chronicled three clear stages in European prehistory. The first was a barbaric stage, followed by a matriarchy, which in turn was followed by a partriarchy.

Bachofen called the barbaric stage *hetairism*, from *hetaira* (companion), which in turn comes from the Greek *hetero* meaning *both*. In this earliest stage, neither males nor females were dominant in society. This was a period of disorder and widespread sexual promiscuity, when children did not know their fathers, women were defenseless, rape took the place of marriage, and family life was virtually nonexistent. Bachofen considered the Greek goddess Aphrodite as the promiscuous goddess of sexual love, with no aspect of order or morality.

And when his thinking is applied to the Norse context of the above myth, the tale speaks on two levels. The first is that universal level of competition and individuation with respect to fathers and sons. The second is a consideration of the brutal and violent hetairism of the earliest history, wherein not only would a son not recognize his father, but the violence of the society would be characterized by the younger men displacing their elders.

In the next phase of European prehistory, Bachofen believed that women banded together for their own defense, which led to the development of a matriarchal society. This phase saw the first blossom of civilization, laws, agriculture, and the arts. Love of the mother and worship of a mother goddess were characteristic of this age, which was symbolized for Bachofen by Demeter, the Greek goddess of agriculture, whom we will discuss further later in this book.

This stage was then followed by the patriarchy, which colors the myth of Phaëthon that follows. Indeed, this context of myths as a "history of prehistory" will prove useful throughout our consideration of the myths, and also sets the stage for the story of Phaëthon, who seeks proof that he is truly his father's son.

PHAËTHON
(Greece and Rome)

This is a tale about fathers and sons that again conveys a truth through paradox—the nature of identity in the father–son relationship—as well as an insight into how ancient Greeks once described natural phenomena by attributing them to the numinous.

Phaëthon was the mortal son of Helios Apollo (Roman: Sol), the sun god, by the woman Clymene. The young boy was ridiculed when he told people that he was the son of Helios, so he decided to prove it to them. Phaëthon slowly climbed up the steep trail leading to the palace of the sun god. He would ask a favor of his father to show the world that he was truly Helios's son.

Helios asked Phaëthon, "Why have you come to see me, son?" Phaëthon explained, "Clymene, my mother, tells me that you are my father, and indeed you greet me as your son, but I need a sign, some proof. No one believes it when I tell them."

Helios replied that Clymene had certainly told the truth—Phaëthon's golden hair was one sure sign of his paternity. So the sun god swore by the lake (whereby the very gods swear their oaths) that whatever Phaëthon asked, Helios would grant.

Phaëthon made a bold request. As Helios's son, Phaëthon requested that his father allow him to drive the sun chariot across the heavens just once.

Helios was horrified. "Of all the many, many things that you could ask of me, this is the only one I would deny you! My sun chariot regulates the days. All the cosmos relies on me to drive that chariot, which no other god, not even great Zeus [Roman: Jupiter] himself, would dare to do! You are a boy—a half-mortal boy, not a god—and you ask me the one thing I shudder to grant you. You have no idea what you are asking!"

The son responded, "But you gave an oath!"

Helios wrinkled his forehead, pursed his lips, and closed his eyes in thought. Haltingly, he said, "Son, let me tell you about the trip, and then you may decide wisely, I think, to ask for something else. You have no idea how hard a trip it is. First, even with all my experience and skill, I have a difficult time getting the winged horses to make the ascent into the sky. And the ascent has to be at precisely the right arc. It requires my total concentration, no matter how many times I have done it. And that, Phaëthon, is hardly the most difficult part of the trip."

Helios continued, "Once you're aloft, things get even more difficult. As many times as I have made the trip, I just can't bear to look down at the earth and see the world below without feeling a little bit dizzy. But look down I must, as the gods know that I see all things, and they regularly ask for a report. I am a god and have done this for a very long time—and still I feel fear. The responsibility is hard to bear. Every living thing depends on my ability to drive the chariot along just the right path. Too close in and the earth will burn; too far out and the earth will freeze. Not only do the living things rely on me to drive the chariot carefully, I must do it in such a way that people go about their business without even thinking of my journey. And that's not the worst of it!

"Once you are up in the heavens, you have to steer so carefully to avoid the fierce beasts that live in the constellations— Leo the Lion will roar at you; you can't let him distract you. Then there is Scorpio, who will threaten you with his pincers. But even if you pass by them without incident, there is plenty of danger left.

"The descent is particularly terrifying, and you must be absolutely sure that the horses go at the precise speed so that the sun chariot does not crash into the sea or the earth, but eases gently into the west, between the posts. To do this, you have to know how to hold the reins and tug at them at just the right time and with just the right amount of force. If you tug too lightly, the horses will crash. Too hard, and they will rear up. Now, Phaëthon, ask me something sensible. Ask me for anything on the earth, in the sky, or below the sea and I will gladly give it to you. But please don't ask to drive my chariot; it will mean your very death!"

But Phaëthon was stubborn and said, "You gave me your word! You promised! You swore an oath! If I am *really* your son, I will be able to do it! Please let me drive the sun chariot. Please!"

Helios began to find this tiresome. "Yes, I *am* your father, and yes, I have taken an oath. Now listen to me—one last time: you have no idea what you are asking for, and I beg you to make another request."

Phaëthon was as adamant as ever. "Father, you promised; you gave your sacred oath. My only wish is to drive your sun chariot across the heavens but once. *Other* fathers let their sons help them with their work. *Other* sons try their hand at the father's trade."

Helios pleaded and pleaded, but to no avail. Helios's heart ached. But Phaëthon only gazed at the beautiful, gleaming sun chariot that had been built by Hephaestus (Roman: Vulcan), the blacksmith of the gods. The chariot had axles, poles, and wheels of the purest gold; gleaming jewels reflected a blinding light. The whole thing shone . . . like the sun! Phaëthon was insensible to his father's words.

The hours were moving along and Helios resigned himself to keep his promise. He covered Phaëthon's face with balm to keep the boy from being burned. In the sky, the stars had begun to scatter and the morning star began its journey home for the daylight. The "rosy fingers of dawn" (Homer) began to lift the cover of night in the east. Phaëthon grew excited and leapt into the chariot, taking the reins, even as the winged horses impatiently stomped their hooves.

Helios offered his son one last warning. "Try to see the wheel tracks of my previous rides and stick right to them. Don't go too high or too low. Remember, *in medio tutissimus ibis:* the middle course is always best. There is a course that avoids both the North and South Poles, and it is clearly marked; please stay on it! All I can do now is to ask Fortune to look after you."

Off went the chariot! The horses, used to Helios's weight and not the light weight of a mere boy, veered off course and zigzagged back and forth until Phaëthon was dizzy. At last, Phaëthon saw his father's wheel tracks and tried to stay in them, but he had no experience using the reins. The cold northern stars were singed by the heat of the sun chariot and went to bathe themselves in the sea, which caused the ocean to overflow, inundating the land. The World Serpent, usually sluggish in its home in the cold southern sea, was awakened by the heat and roared in fury, frightening even the gods. Phaëthon was terrified and jerked the reins, which sent the horses racing upward toward the terrible creatures in the constellations. The Scorpion narrowly missed Phaëthon's head with its pincers, and the frightened boy again jerked the reins, sending the horses downward. The chariot then passed too close to the earth, igniting forests and causing entire rivers (including the Nile) to boil away. The snow on the mountaintops then melted, drowning the valleys below. Paralyzed with fear, Phaëthon dropped the reins.

The horses sped on, off course, into the far reaches of space. Phaëthon looked down to see the world in flames far below him and was terrified. He began to breathe in the flames and lost consciousness. His blond hair caught fire. The parched ground cracked open, exposing Pluto (Roman: Dis) in the underworld where the dead dwelled. Poseidon (Roman: Neptune), god of the sea, three times tried to lift his head above the waves to see what was going on, but it was too hot for him to bear!

The gods despaired at what was taking place. If the earth were to burn, what point would there be in being a god? How would the gods survive if humans were killed, if there were no crops for the sacrifices, no incense for the ceremonies, and nothing to rule? Mother Earth appeared to be dying. All the

gods, fond as they were of Helios, called out to Zeus to stop
Phaëthon before it was too late.

For all his bluster and thunder, Zeus was softhearted. He
could hardly bear to kill his own nephew, a mere boy, the son
of the well-beloved Helios. Things had gone too far by now; he
had no choice. The clouds were burning up, and without
clouds there would be no rain to quench the fires. Zeus had to
act now or perish himself. So he launched a lightning bolt that
hit the chariot, causing it to crash to earth, killing Phaëthon.
To this day, when you see a falling star, it is to remind you of
the story of Phaëthon. Of course, you see falling stars only at
night. Zeus did this out of sympathy for Helios, who is out
during the day.

So many animals and plants died in the conflagration that
Zeus had to muster the few remaining clouds together to make
it rain, which slowly quenched the flames and allowed the sur-
viving world to replenish itself over time. The cosmos had narrowly escaped total destruction, all because a boy wanted to
impress his friends.

Connections

The story of Phaëthon is a multifaceted presentation of
critical issues not only in the father-son dynamic, but in the
basic human conditions of identity, finitude, and estrangement. As stated before, there are perennial parental issues of
love versus indulgence and the dilemma of keeping a promise
to one's child, even when keeping the promise can hurt
the child. But there are still more, still deeper truth-bearing
paradoxes.

There is, of course, the paradox of the son trying to establish

an independent identity through brave exploits while simultaneously laying claim to his identity as his father's son. There is
the brash, overconfident youth in search of great exploits to
establish an identity counterpoised against the wise, compe-
tent, and tempered father. There is also the universal paradox
of the son challenging the father, all the while seeking the
father's approval. But there is a more critical issue of identity
that applies to us all.

Phaëthon, the son of a god and a mortal woman, sets out to
find who he is and cannot accept the limits—the finitude—
inherent in the answer. For the son of a god and a mortal is
himself mortal and finite. He cannot see himself as a whole.

Our faith traditions, especially in the West and in India,
speak of the human as being variously "created in the image of
God" or "bearing a spark of the Divine Self"—but as mortal
and not a god. Yet as we lay claim to God as our "father," we
often assert the right to be God, to "play God." This can bear
the seeds of self-destruction, or even destruction of the human
race. (For example, atomic power was first explained to many
simply as "harnessing the power of the sun.") And thus, we
are Phaëthon. But in asserting that "we are God" or can "play
God," we lose our humanity. We ache to believe in the fatherhood of God, and seek proofs of our connection to the numinous, but refusing to accept our own finitude is only to our
own peril: it was positivism that took up Helios's reins.

Also, note that it was difficult for Zeus to kill Phaëthon.
Divine justice indulges youths in their exploits until order is
threatened.

The tale of Phaëthon is one of the tales of nature and
human nature that we see so often in the myths and will
explore in greater depth later in this book. On one level, this is
an obvious nature myth regarding the origin of falling stars

and how the sun moves east to west through the heavens. It is about both the cosmos and our place in the cosmos. It is about fathers and sons, the relationship between humans and the numinous, and our arrogance in not accepting our finitude. Yet, it may also be a history of prehistory.

This myth (and others) may be historic records of a horrible conflagration and drought that shook the world; some believe that it was caused by an asteroid that hit the earth. The Chinese have a myth about a year when twelve suns appeared in the sky, causing lakes and rivers to dry up until things were put right. And as Gerhard Herm wrote in *The Celts*,

> In the second half of the fifteenth century B.C. the whole world experienced a series of disasters such as have never since been recorded. It began with a fall in the water table to seven meters, with the result that springs dried up, rivers became trickles, bogs stopped growing. This drought was preceded by a climatic optimum that went on for thousands of years with long summers and mild winters. . . . Vines grew in southern Norway, the whole of Scandinavia lived in the shadow of mixed and deciduous forest, there were glaciers only in the extreme north. These times are probably recalled in the Greek saga of *Phaeton.*

GRANDFATHER, FATHER, AND SON
(Algonquin)

The Algonquin–speaking nations of North America stretched from the Atlantic coast to the Great Plains and included such tribes as the New England Abenaki; the Virginia Powhatans and Potomacks; the Great Lakes Chippewa and Ottawa; and the Sauk at their gateway to the west. Even in their cooperative, communal society, one found tensions between individual and group identity, and the impetuousness of sons in establishing a separate identity from their fathers.

Once, in a certain village there lived three generations of warrior-hunters. The eldest was Grandfather, a wise and respected elder who had lived between seventy and eighty summers. His son was Father, who had earned the right to be respected as an elder through his courage and the wisdom of living more than fifty summers. And then there was Son, a little over twenty summers old and totally consumed with making a name for himself.

Son, however, had neither hunted nor fished, having concentrated instead on making his name as a great warrior. The problem was that there hadn't been any wars this particular year, and Son knew that there was not enough preserved fish or meats to get him and his wife through the winter. Although Son didn't have to worry—no one ever went without in the village, as it was the people's custom to share—each family also wanted to be certain that it had enough of their own food supply. Besides, the people of the village also had a great deal of respect for those skilled in hunting. Son was concerned that asking for help would constitute an admission that he had neither hunted nor fished; it would ruin his reputation. So he went into the woods to ask Otter for help in fishing.

Otter, the most skilled fisherman in the forest, replied, "I could help you with fishing, but why ask *my* help? Your grandfather is the wisest and best fisherman in the village, and certainly he could teach you how to fish . . . although we both know that he has already tried to teach you, but you were too busy with your dreams of glory. Why not tell the villagers that you lack enough meat, and you care only about your reputation. You are a fool!" With a splash, Otter swam away to do his own fishing.

Son then consulted Wolf, the greatest hunter. Wolf said, "I could teach you all of the secrets of hunting, but I won't. Everyone knows that your father is one of the most skilled of hunters; why not ask him? But I recall that your father has often tried to teach you to hunt, and you were only interested in gaining a great name as a glorious warrior. Moreover, there are plenty of people in the village who are more than happy to share their meat with you. So you really don't have a problem. You are a foooooool!" howled the wolf as it ran away.

Son then consulted hardworking Beaver, who knew more than anyone about getting through the winter. Beaver had been busy building his dam and preparing it to keep his family warm, safe, and dry through the long winter. Before Son could say even one word, Beaver said, "You are a fool! I will be safe and warm this winter because I worked and worked all year long. Your grandfather has lived more than seventy winters and your father through more than fifty; ask their advice." But Son felt that his grandfather and father would think less of him for asking for help.

Son then cried out to the Great Spirit, the Grandfather and Father of all things, who responded by saying nothing. Why? Because the Great Spirit had already answered Son and seen to it that all of his needs, and those of his family, would be well met. Son heard the rushing of the wind through the trees, which seemed to say, "Come back when your eyes are open to the obvious."

Despairing and ashamed, Son went to Grandfather, asking the old man to teach him to fish. Upon hearing this, Grandfather rolled his eyes and said, "Haven't I already taught you to fish? Oh, I tried and tried, but you were too bored to learn."

But as he loved his grandson, he continued, "Well, my eye-sight is too poor to hunt deer anymore, and my hand isn't quite steady enough to spear fish—but nobody can surpass me with a hook and line." But when Son and Grandfather went fishing, Otter decided to teach Son a lesson. He chased all of the fish to Grandfather's hook and line, and only two pathetic-looking little minnows to Son's line. To Son, this was more humiliating than catching no fish at all! So Son carried Grand-father's overflowing basket of fish into the village, making sure that people could see him with the catch. Then Grand-father, tired from his long day, went to his lodge to rest.

With Grandfather asleep, Son took the basket of fish into the center of the village and announced, "I am the greatest of all fishermen with a hook and line! Look, I have a huge basket of fish. I insist that you take as many fish as you care to, and think of me when you enjoy them this winter." So, the people took fish out of the basket to smoke and store for the winter. The young people of the village were so impressed that they sang praises of Son and his skill as a fisherman. But the old people of the village knew better and just rolled their eyes.

The next day, Son went to Father and asked to go hunting. Father agreed, but pointed out that he had, in fact, tried to teach Son the proper techniques of hunting years ago; the boy had been too distracted to learn. Still, Father took Son into the forest and, with the help of Wolf, shot six deer! Father told Son to preserve the deer by drying and pounding the meat into pemmican to ensure that there would be provisions for the winter. As the cold air had chilled Father's bones, he retired to his lodge to rest.

Son once more went to the center of the village, dragging the six deer on a sled, and announced, "See what a great hunter I am! I have slain six deer. As a token of my largesse, you may keep four of the deer for yourselves!" The young people marveled and sang Son's praises once more, while the old ones snickered in silent amusement.

Now, having demonstrated his prowess as a hunter and fisherman, Son decided that he would truly bring glory upon himself if he killed a bear. His wife was busy preparing the venison and fish for the winter, so he slipped off to kill a bear. He took some meat with him as bait. No sooner did he place the meat on the ground than a whole family of huge bears appeared. As Son prepared to shoot an arrow, he stepped on a twig, causing it to snap loudly. The sound alerted the bears, and they chased Son into a tree. The angry she-bear swiped at Son with her claws, tearing his loincloth from him, leaving him naked and frightened in the tree. She took a second swipe at him and nicked his backside. Son cried out for help, and the villagers came and chased away the bears.

When the villagers saw Son, he looked ridiculous, cowering naked in the tree. They noted the scratch on his bottom and called him Eyes in the Arse, as it was through the she-bear's scratch that Son's eyes were finally opened to see that the village worked on cooperation and there was more honor in doing his day-to-day part than in seeking a reputation as a great warrior and hunter. Son told this story to his sons, and they to theirs. He obtained great glory and respect from the people for many truly great exploits wherein he did not seek glory, but was instead loved for being able to laugh at himself and tell this story.

Connections

My grandmother used to say that "glory is no substitute for dependability," a point generously demonstrated in this

myth. The son sought instant glory that his father and grandfather had earned through hard work and faithful attention to
duty. They had glory and respect as warriors, but they certainly won their places of respect through being faithful mem-
bers of their tribe in mundane tasks. The son, of course, not
only wished to distinguish himself from his father and grandfather, but sought to surpass them without their years of
faithful attention to duty. Youth *seeks* instant rewards, only to
find them elusive; age lives out duty without seeking rewards.
Youth lacks patience, even to learn, and only failure opens the
eyes of youth to reality. The young man sought the instant
approval of the village futilely; the old men had it by merely
fulfilling their duties and being who they were.

We have looked at a fundamental human relationship, that of
fathers and sons. The protective love of the parent is jux-
taposed against the sometimes foolish, rash, and difficult
struggle of the child to establish an individual identity. As
truth is so often contained in paradox, the son is often dependent upon the father to provide the means necessary to establish that individuality. Our process of becoming is always in,
with, and through others.

   We shall now look at this process of becoming in a second
elemental human relationship, that of romantic love. Here the
becoming is a shared process. It is in romantic love that we
see the enormous transforming power of love at work in the
process of becoming.

2. Romantic Love

A second elementary human relationship is that of romantic love—and what do the myths tell us about love? The one thread binding the stories in this chapter is the power of love to *transform*. The German poet Goethe (1749–1832) expressed it best:

Steigt hinan zu höhrem Kreise	Climb onward to a higher circle
Wachset immer unvermerkt,	Without even noticing,
	grow ever as
Wie noch ewig reiner Weise	pure, eternal wisdom in
Gottesgegenwart verstarkt!	God's presence strengthens!
Denn is das der Geister Nahrung	Thus the nutrition of the spirit
Die im freisten Äther waltet:	rules in the freest ether:
Ewigen Liebens Offnungbarung	The eternal revelation of Love
Die zur Seligkeit entfaltet.	carries us off to blessedness.

—Johann Wolfgang von Goethe, *Faust*, Part II, Act V
(Translation, J.F.B.)

In three of the myths, the soul of the beloved is depicted as a butterfly. Of course, a butterfly (and a soul) goes through

metamorphoses, and in each of these stories, love is the catalyst for the metamorphosis. In several of the myths, couples
defy even the gods by loving each other; in others, a woman is
given the choice between a man and a god, and inevitably
chooses the man. The man she meets has a fatal flaw, but he is
not the same man after she loves him. This shows that love
operates on the *real*, yet transforms.

In speaking of the power of love to transform, the myths
remind us that our existence is in, with, and through others.
Love becomes the catalyst for our process of becoming, and
each of the lovers in the myths to follow is not quite the same
at the end of the tale as at the beginning. Indeed, romantic
love is the shared struggle for existence and meaning. This
principle is found in the philosophy of Karl Jaspers
(1883–1969) and Martin Buber (1878–1965): that love is an
indispensable catalyst of our becoming who and what we truly
are meant to be, the means to realization of our quests. Our
process of becoming is with others, and when we are "heroes,"
we realize our quest cannot be done alone. Jaspers uses the
term *loving struggle* to describe the relentless search for truth
shared between people who love each other; each helps the
other find truth and become "their true self," which is what
Jaspers refers to as the realization of God's will. For Buber,
one cannot "become" unless one enters into a life of dialogue;
such a dialogue cannot fully exist (between two people or with
God) unless there is an I-thou relationship of openness and
communication. Love gives meaning to life.

The transforming power of love is a fundamental organizing
theme of the myths—yours, mine, and ours.

NALA AND DAMAYANTI
(India)

S cholars of the diffusionist school of myth believe that there were two strong myth–producing cultural "spheres." The southern sphere stretched from Africa to Polynesia. The northern sphere stretched across the vast Eurasian landmass and included the Norse, Celts, Greeks, and Aryan invaders of north India. As the Aryans invaded India from the north, worshiping gods and speaking a language related to Greece, they encountered the Dravidian peoples of the south, who belonged to the southern myth–producing sphere. The result of this encounter is the extraordinarily rich mythology of India.

One theme in Indian mythology, which appears in this myth and in the Indian national epic, the *Mahabharata*, is the king who loses his realm through a toss of the dice.

Nala was a young king of Nishadha who was known as handsome and skilled in all sixty-four of the arts that a king should know. He was also the world's best and fastest chariot driver and horseman. But, he was lonely, as he had not yet found a suitable bride.

In a nearby kingdom lived King Bhima, whose daughter Damayanti was said to be the most beautiful woman on earth—so beautiful, in fact, that she attracted the attentions of the gods.

Nala used to relax by strolling through the palace gardens. On one such stroll, he saw a beautiful swan and caught it. The swan, begging to be set free, said, "If you let me go, King Nala, I will fly to Damayanti and sing your praises. She will become your bride." At this, Nala let the swan go, and it immediately flew to the palace of King Bhima.

Appearing before the beautiful Damayanti, the swan spoke of the prince's handsomeness, wisdom, talents, and skill. "Nala is the fairest of men and you are the fairest of women; you should marry each other." To which Damayanti replied, "Don't tell me this. Go tell Nala!" For she had already decided that it was Nala whom she wished to marry.

King Bhima himself was eager to see his daughter contract a proper royal marriage and was planning a *swayamvara*, the banquet where princes were brought as suitors before a princess. The chosen suitor would have a garland placed around his neck. No one, not even the gods, could deny a princess her choice of husband at a *swayamvara*. But, while waiting to hear word back from Nala, Damayanti began to grieve and stopped eating. The situation became so grave that King Bhima decided to hurry the preparations for the *swayamvara* and dispatched his servants to provide invitations to all manner of kings, princes, and even gods.

The god Narada spent one of his earthly sojourns in King Bhima's realm and had heard of the beauty of Damayanti. He quickly flew up to heaven to tell Indra, master of lightning, of the beautiful princess and her coming *swayamvara*. Indra was himself in a particularly foul mood; the kings of the earth had stopped making their customary offerings to him.

The gods themselves discussed Damayanti, and four gods decided to attend the *swayamvara* as suitors: Indra (who controls thunder and lightning), Agni (who controls fire), Varuna (who controls the vault of the heavens), and Yama (lord of the dead). They all set out together for Bhima's court, with plenty of good-natured teasing about whom Damayanti would choose. They were also keenly aware that Damayanti wanted only Nala.

En route, the gods met Nala and told him to go to Damayanti with a message. Nala was to tell Damayanti in person that four gods were on their way to seek her hand. Nala was sick with love for Damayanti and prayed to all of the gods to have this duty lifted from him. But Nala was faithful to the gods. And beyond the many gods, of course, is the Eternal Brahma, who is so great and so intent on the good that what is painful for men or even gods can be brought to good purposes.

Nala went before Damayanti. Upon seeing Nala, Damayanti's heart raced with joy; she was sure that he could have come only to propose marriage. But instead he conveyed his message, doing what the gods had asked of him. He told Damayanti, "I stand before you because the gods asked me to do so; piety demanded it. I am here to tell you that four gods are on their way to ask your hand in marriage. Now that I have done my duty, I will also tell you that I am in love with you and plan to appear at the *swayamvara* as a suitor on my own behalf. You know that I will accept whatever choice you make."

Damayanti, deeply moved, replied, "It is you and only you, Nala, whom I love; it is you that I will marry."

Nala responded, "We both love each other. But who are we to go against the gods? They could destroy us in a minute!"

Yet knowing that even the gods must obey the choice of a princess at a *swayamvara*, Damayanti remained insistent. "It is you, Nala, whom I will marry and no other."

When the day of the *swayamvara* arrived, the gods did appear—all in the guise of Nala! So, Damayanti stood facing five physical Nalas, but loving only the true Nala. She looked intently at each of them and found it was easy to identify the real Nala: he was nervous! Perspiration beaded on his forehead, his hands were shaking, and his mouth appeared dry. She quickly placed the garland around Nala's neck and declared that he alone would be her husband. For, given a choice between a god and a man, a woman will always take a man.

The gods, including the rejected suitors, were all very happy. The Eternal One had a lesson for them all, and it was wonderful to see two people so much in love. The lesson was this: Love is stronger than lightning (Indra), stronger than fire (Agni), so strong that it could bridge the vault of heaven (Varuna), and even stronger than death (Yama). All of the gods gave Nala and Damayanti beautiful wedding presents and many blessings.

However, Kali, the demon of the fourth age, was not part of these festivities. She immediately sought to destroy this happy scene. In her opinion, it was ridiculous for a mortal woman to choose a man over the gods. While the gods tried in vain to persuade Kali otherwise, Kali was determined to destroy Nala and Damayanti. Kali appointed her minion, Dvapara, to keep an eye on Nala in order to find a fatal flaw that could be exploited.

It so happened that Nala, after twelve long years of Dvapara's observation, made a trivial mistake in the observance of a ritual; this removed some of Nala's divine protection and gave Kali the desired opening. Kali had also learned that Nala liked to gamble. So Kali took possession of Nala and turned him into a compulsive gambler. In this condition, Nala challenged his brother, Pushkara, to a "friendly" game of dice.

They sat down and gambled for months until Nala had lost

his entire royal treasury to his brother. No one in the court, not even Damayanti, could stop Nala from gambling. One day Pushkara suggested that they gamble with Damayanti as the stakes. Yet this was one thing that Nala would not bet, so he put up the kingdom instead. When he lost, Nala surrendered his crown and was sent into exile by his cruel brother.

Damayanti faithfully followed Nala into exile, and they had spent six days on the road, hungry, when they paused to rest. All that Nala had left was his own cloak. With his stomach growling, Nala spotted a flock of birds and decided to snare them to get something to eat. Damayanti's clothes were badly tattered, so Nala ripped his cloak in half, using half to cover his wife and the other half to snare the birds. Just as it appeared that he would catch them, the birds flew away with the cloak, sneering, "Don't you recognize us, Nala? We are the dice! We could not rest until we had taken everything, even your last stitch of clothing." And then Nala—naked, hungry, and despairing—sat down and wept. He told Damayanti that she was free to leave him; he had ruined her life.

But Damayanti replied, "You defied even the gods to marry me. You refused to gamble with me as the stakes. I love you and can never leave you." Damayanti suggested that they go to her father's court to live. But, although he had lost everything else, Nala still had his pride, and he knew the humiliation of appearing naked and hungry before his in-laws would be more than he could bear. They walked on until they found an abandoned hovel to shelter them for the night.

When Damayanti had fallen asleep, Nala found a rusty sword. He cut off a small piece of the remaining garment that Damayanti was wearing and fashioned himself a loincloth. He then set out on his own, as he wanted to spare Damayanti any further pain. He thought it better to leave now than face her father, destitute as he was. He tried to leave twice, and twice he returned; the third time he just kept on walking.

Damayanti awoke to find her husband gone; she began to weep. She scoured the forest in search of Nala, but without a sign. As she cared more for Nala's well-being than her own, she cried out to the gods that she would gladly take ten times Nala's portion of suffering on herself if only it gave her husband some relief.

As she was wandering, a giant serpent seized her. A brave hunter happened upon the scene and slew the beast. The hunter now asked for Damayanti's body as his reward. Damayanti called out, "Listen, O gods! If I am faithful to Nala, this hunter shall certainly die." And the hunter fell dead that very second.

Damayanti continued onward, and with the protection of the gods, she walked unharmed among the serpents and wild beasts. She came to an ashram where the *rishis*, or holy men, secreted themselves from the world. They welcomed her and listened as she told her sad story. The holy men assured her that, after some trials, she would be reunited with her husband. Then she fell asleep, only to wake and find the ashram and the *rishis* had disappeared.

After a fortnight, she encountered a caravan of traders and told them her story. They agreed to give her food and shelter for the night. However, a herd of wild elephants stampeded in the night, killing many people and wrecking the camp. The traders blamed Damayanti for the calamity and left her behind.

However, the traders had told Damayanti that they were on their way to the court of King Subahu in Shedi. She followed the tracks of the caravan and found herself at the very palace of Subahu, where a curious thing took place. Royalty often has an uncanny ability to recognize other royalty, even when they appear as shabby beggars. The queen of Shedi knew that Damayanti was of royal blood and took her into her home until Damayanti could travel back to King Bhima's court.

Meanwhile, Nala had survived, but he had endured his own trials. Wandering through the forests, Nala saw a blazing circle of fire and heard a voice crying out for help. He bravely ran through the flames and rescued a *naga*, one of the royal serpents endowed with magical powers. The serpent then chose an odd way to demonstrate his gratitude: he bit Nala. But with the bite came a great blessing. It changed Nala's appearance into that of a different person. The *naga* explained that this would confuse Kali and ensure his reunion with Damayanti.

The *naga* told Nala of Ritruparna, king of Ajodhya, who was a skilled gambler whose success with dice was celebrated throughout India. Now, much as Nala had no luck with dice, Ritruparna had absolutely no skill whatever with horses and chariots. So the *naga* told Nala to go to Ritruparna and use his extraordinary horsemanship skills to work as a chariot driver. The *naga* shrewdly suggested that Nala then find an appropriate time wherein Nala could exchange his skills as a charioteer with Ritruparna's gambling skills. Finally, the *naga* gave Nala a magic cloak that would allow Nala to reassume his previous form.

On yet another front, King Bhima had grown very worried about his now-returned daughter and very disgusted with his wastrel son-in-law. Bhima now sent messengers in all directions to find him. The messengers were to ask, "Where are you, gambler, who left your wife nothing but a half a cloak?" Only Nala would understand the question, and if anyone did answer, the messenger was to race back to King Bhima.

The messengers arrived in Ajodhya and made their in-
quiries. When they were prepared to give up, they asked King
Ritruparna's chariot driver, a man called Vahuka, the question. The chariot driver became very animated, his eyes welled
up with tears, and he praised the faithfulness of a good
woman—her willingness to forgive, to share hardship, and
still remain in love. The messengers remembered what Nala
looked like, and Vahuka was quite a different-looking man.
But this was the first response they had heard, and they raced
back to Bhima to give their report.

The messengers informed Bhima and Damayanti that one
man, a charioteer named Vahuka, had responded to their
question. Unsure whether this Vahuka and Nala could be
the same person, Damayanti decided to offer a test. She had
the messengers inform the court of Ritruparna that she, now
presumably widowed, would have a second *swayamvara*. Although there truly was to be no *swayamvara*, this would help
her at last find Nala, if he were still alive.

Ritruparna was unmarried and had heard of Damayanti's
great beauty. He called his charioteer and explained that
Damayanti would again hold a *swayamvara* to select a new
husband. Nala was both delighted to hear that Damayanti
was alive and, strengthened by the *naga*'s magic, eager to
make his own case that he was truly her husband. Ritruparna
got into his chariot and ordered Vahuka to drive as fast as possible to Bhima's court. Ritruparna was amazed at his charioteer's skill and the great speed at which the horses traveled,
and praised Vahuka. As they whizzed past a mango tree,
Ritruparna told Vahuka that there were exactly 150 mangoes
on the ground and 50,000,000 leaves and 1095 ripening mangoes still on the tree. This was amazing. Ritruparna's knowledge of numbers was unlike anything Nala had ever seen. He

stopped the chariot and began counting. Ritruparna had been absolutely correct.

Now, remembering the *naga*'s prophecy, Nala offered to exchange his skills as the swiftest charioteer in the land for Ritruparna's skill with numbers. As Ritruparna had always desired the ability to drive chariots well, he agreed. Ritruparna added that while this skill with numbers made him invincible as a gambler, it was now tiresome. As the *naga* had also prophesied, with this new skill, Nala was entirely free of Kali's curse.

When the two reached Bhima's court, they were both dismayed to see no evidence that a *swayamvara* was to take place. Bhima then asked Ritruparna why he had traveled such a distance. Embarrassed, Ritruparna responded, "Merely to convey my greetings to a fellow king." Bhima thought this very odd and he was suspicious. Damayanti was also confused as, hearing the reports from the messengers, she fully expected her husband to come through the doors. When she saw the chariot driver, she was bitterly disappointed. However, as Vahuka had answered the question, it appeared that he must have some knowledge of Nala, and so Damayanti ordered the messengers to interrogate him one more time.

When they did, it was more than Vahuka could bear. He gave the same answer as before, but began weeping upon seeing his twin children born in his absence—Indra and Indrasen—approach him and then run away as though he were a stranger. This was reported back to Damayanti. She then summoned the charioteer to appear before her for questioning. "What do you know of Nala?" Vahuka answered, "Only Nala can tell you of Nala!"

Upon hearing this, Damayanti wondered for the first time whether this might be Nala in disguise. She asked him again.

He swept the cloak that the *naga* had given him over his head and regained his old appearance, much to the joy of everyone. Now he was prepared to regain his throne.

Nala appeared at his former palace, where his brother Pushkara now ruled. He asked to see his brother, who greeted him with, "Haven't you lost enough?" Then Pushkara challenged him to a game of dice with Damayanti as the stakes. With his new skill, Nala instead suggested that they play for their very lives; the loser would die. Pushkara, recalling his brother's previously bad luck and not wishing to have a possible rival contender to the throne, hastily agreed. When Nala won, Pushkara expected to die.

Instead of punishing Pushkara, the generous Nala gave his brother a neighboring kingdom to rule. As the *naga* had prophesied, all had been not only restored to Nala, but increased many times over.

Connections

The core message of this story is to be found in Brahma's lesson to the gods at the first *swayamvara*: Love is stronger than Indra's lightning, burns hotter than Agni's fire, can bridge the vault of Varuna's heavens, and is even stronger than Yama (death). This story is about the strength of romantic love, the process of transformation brought about by love, and the process of "becoming" that every human being experiences. Our process of becoming cannot take place in isolation; love is always its transforming catalyst.

Jaspers's doctrine of the loving struggle is clearly illustrated in the story of Nala and Damayanti, wherein true love bears all—addiction, material loss, separation, and other trials. But the love does not merely bear or withstand these trials, it is both defined and refined by them. Nala and Damayanti certainly understand the meaning of *for richer, for poorer*. The power of their love to transform Nala, and not merely the intervention of the *naga* serpent, is what breaks the curse of Kali.

The symbolism inherent in both the swan as messenger and the *naga* serpent merit our attention. The swan appears often in the myths as a messenger, and in this myth, as in Irish mythology, the swan is a messenger of love; it speaks of a love that already existed in Nala and Damayanti's deeper selves. It is interesting to note that to the Jungian, water is symbolic of our depths, our unconscious, and the swan is at home in the three realms of water, land, and sky. Also, the swan appears in the creation myths of the Dene (Navajo), Algonquins, and Buryat Mongols in the role of assisting the Creator. This appears to speak to the dawn of consciousness, just as Nala and Damayanti's swan awakens them to an awareness of feelings they had already had.

The *naga* serpent as well is symbolic. The magic that the *naga* provides to Nala appears to be symbolic of a new power within Nala that enables him to break his addiction, regain his kingdom, and be reunited with Damayanti. Love is the catalyst of that new power.

As is often the case in the love myths, love is put to a final test before the lovers are reunited. As in the Greek story of Odysseus, Nala returns in disguise to his own home, unrecognized by even his own children. Much as Odysseus had to battle the suitors of his wife, Penelope, Nala arrives ostensibly for a *swayamvara*, where Damayanti's new suitors are expected to gather. This use of disguise and change of identity is full of meaning; Nala is not really Vahuka, but neither is he the old Nala. He has *become* the man we see at the end of the story, transformed by love.

That is because Nala's struggle for existence, his process of becoming is in, with, and through Damayanti. Having lost his kingdom and having fled in shame from his beloved, Nala had a quest: to free himself from his addiction, become a man worthy to be a king, and be united with Damayanti. The power of this transformation is in love: that of Nala for Damayanti, and her love for him.

APHRODITE AND HER MANY FACES
(Greece, Rome, and Germany)

The Greek goddess of beauty was Aphrodite (Roman: Venus), whose name means *foam-born*. As depicted in Botticelli's painting *Birth of Venus*, the goddess was conceived in a rather unconventional manner. The god Cronus castrated his father Uranus (which means *Heaven*) and threw his genitals into the sea, where they produced sea foam, whence sprang Aphrodite, fully grown and riding on her emblem, the scallop shell. (The Indian goddess of both beauty and prosperity, Lakshmi, arose in a similar manner from the sea.) From her Greek name, we have the word *aphrodisiac*, quite descriptive of her function in myth.

The Infidelity of Aphrodite
(Greece)

Aphrodite was one of the three great goddesses of the Greeks, along with Hera (Roman: Juno), the wife of Zeus (Roman: Jupiter) and patroness of childbirth, and Athena (Roman: Minerva), the goddess of wisdom. Indeed, the Greeks considered her a "foreign" goddess, with her origins variously given in Asia

Minor and Cyprus. In the Trojan War, Aphrodite favored the Trojans, and Athena the Greeks, so it was said that while the Greeks fought their adversaries with wisdom, it was Troy that fought with passion.

Once, Helios (Roman: Sol), the sun god, was driving his chariot across the heavens and happened to catch Ares (Roman: Mars), the god of war, and Aphrodite in flagrante delicto on the bed intended for Aphrodite and her husband Hephaestus (Roman: Vulcan), the lame smith of the gods. Helios then passed this information on to the cuckolded husband, who was understandably outraged.

This was no isolated incident; Ares and Aphrodite had been carrying on an affair for some time, to the bewilderment of the gods. The gods of Olympus disliked the bloodthirsty, avaricious, power-mad, cruel Ares and avoided associating with him; how could the beautiful Aphrodite be attracted to such a nasty god? In time, Aphrodite bore Ares three children. The two boys were Phobos (fear) and Deimos (dread); the girl was Harmonia.

Hephaestus wanted to catch his wife in the unfaithful act, so he told Aphrodite that he was going to Lemnos for a little rest. Aphrodite watched out the window until her husband was out of sight and then beckoned Ares to join her. Now, Hephaestus, as smith to the gods, had forged an elaborate net of bronze that was very strong, but so artfully made that it resembled cloth. He had attached the net to the bedposts in hopes to ensnare his wife and her lover—and that he did. Hephaestus gathered together a company of gods to go with him and found the adulterous pair naked and wrapped up in his net. (The goddesses did not come with them, as the whole issue was scandalous.) The gods relished the chance to both see the hated Ares compromised and the beautiful Aphrodite naked.

Poseidon (Roman: Neptune), the sea god, was smitten at the sight of naked Aphrodite. He had his own prurient thoughts, but decided to feign a grand gesture and pretended to be sympathetic to the wronged Hephaestus. Poseidon suggested that Ares make restitution for his misdeed by paying Hephaestus the equivalent of the bride-price that the smith had given to Zeus for Aphrodite. If Ares didn't pay up, Poseidon offered to do the honorable thing: allow Hephaestus to divorce his adulterous wife, and marry Aphrodite himself! Hephaestus failed to see through this ploy, and expressed appreciation for Poseidon's chivalry.

Ares never did pay up, but Hephaestus, for all of his anger and dismay, remained too much in love to divorce Aphrodite, so Poseidon never could follow through with his promise. And, as Aphrodite could renew her virginity by bathing in the sea, she was not prepared to give up recreational sex.

Still, Zeus became disgusted by Aphrodite's habitual promiscuity and decided to teach her a lesson. He caused her to fall in love with a mortal, Anchises. When Aphrodite appeared to Anchises in the guise of a mortal princess, he, too, fell head over heels in love. After they had spent the night together, Aphrodite turned to Anchises and revealed her true identity.

Anchises now shook with fear and dread. He knew there was a terrible price to pay for seeing a goddess naked; sleeping with her could only be worse.

Indeed, Zeus did decide to hurl a thunderbolt at Anchises. But, just as it was about to strike, Aphrodite placed her magic girdle (which causes everyone to fall in love with the wearer) in front of Anchises to deflect the bolt. Anchises survived, but was never able to walk again. Later Aphrodite bore him a son, Aeneas, the hero of Troy.

The Judgment of Paris
(Greece)

Thetis and Peleus were to be married and all of the gods were invited to the wedding, except one: Eris, goddess of discord and sister of Ares. Of course, discord is the last thing one wants at a wedding feast. Nonetheless, she had been slighted and decided to get even. So she crafted a golden apple, inscribed it with the words *For the Fairest*, and tossed it into the banquet hall. More than one goddess laid claim to it: Hera, the wife of Zeus; Athena, the goddess of wisdom and patroness of Athens; and, of course, Aphrodite. The three began to quarrel and turned to Zeus for a judgment. It would have been folly for Zeus to offer any opinion. His wife Hera could not be disappointed; Athena, as his daughter, could not be disappointed; and, of course, as the goddess of beauty, Aphrodite was entitled to the apple as well. So, characteristically, Zeus gave the decision to a mortal: Paris, son of King Priam of Troy.

The goddesses were not above bribery to win the apple. Athena promised to make Paris invincible in battle; Hera offered him the mastery of all Asia; and Aphrodite, reading Paris's mind, used feminine wiles. She loosened her robe to offer Paris a tantalizing glimpse of her cleavage and then promised Paris that she would give him the most beautiful woman in the world. And so, Aphrodite won the apple, and Paris married Helen of Troy.

The real winners in the contest, however, were Eris and her cruel brother, who sowed the seeds of a bloody war between

Greece and Troy that began as a result of Helen's and Paris's love. Athena and Hera were so angry that they took the side of the Greeks, who as we now know were victorious. Aphrodite sided with the Trojans. Even after the war persisted, Hera tormented Aphrodite and Anchises' son Aeneas (see page 194).

Cupid and Psyche
(Rome)

The story of Cupid (Greek: Eros) and Psyche comes to us from the Roman poet Ovid's *Metamorphoses*, and thus, the Latin names of the gods are used. Ovid (43 B.C.–A.D. 17) wrote a great deal about love and, per the word *metamorphoses*, love's power to transform. Ovid and this story represent a marked cultural change in Rome. Early Rome was singularly unromantic, sober, austere, and martial. Ovid's Rome, Imperial Rome, saw the blossoming of poetry, the result of prosperity and increased leisure.

Once there was a king with three beautiful daughters, the fairest of whom was Psyche, the youngest. Her name means both *soul* and *butterfly* in Greek. Her beauty was such that the entire world soon knew of her and men swooned at the very mention of her name. Not only was she physically beautiful, but she was a kind and innocent girl as well. Soon people began to compare her with Venus (Greek: Aphrodite), the goddess of beauty. In time, the temples of Venus were ignored; no one brought sacrifices or invoked the name of the goddess for help. For, as the people saw it, Venus was a distant goddess who lived on Mount Olympus, while the very picture of beauty, Psyche, lived in their midst.

Venus became very angry about the attention given to a mere mortal girl, and she called her son Cupid (Greek: Eros)

to assist in solving the problem. The arrows of Cupid are irresistible and invincible: anyone they strike falls hopelessly in
love. Venus decided that a fitting punishment would be for
Cupid to cause the vilest, ugliest man on earth to fall in love
with Psyche.

Upon inspecting the situation for himself, Cupid fell head
over heels in love with Psyche and forgot all about his mother's
commands. Venus took the silence of her son as assent that he
would do her bidding, and was certain that the matter would be
taken care of promptly.

But as time passed, Psyche was left unloved by any man.
Men still looked at her in passing and praised her beauty, but
that was that. Not a single suitor approached her. Her two sisters had married well, while this most beautiful of mortals
appeared to be headed for a lonely spinsterhood. Her parents
despaired and decided to seek the advice of the god Apollo at
Delphi. Of course, Apollo (who now was the master of the sun
chariot) had seen and known all about both Psyche and
Cupid.

Apollo himself had a reputation for his taste in beautiful
mortal women, but he was also the brother of Venus and did
not wish to incur her wrath. So, speaking through the oracle,
he diplomatically told the parents that Psyche would indeed
have a lover—a horrible winged serpent. The parents were
advised to take her up to a lonely rock to meet her lover, who
was as strong as the gods and could not be resisted.

Sadly, her father obeyed this advice and left the beautiful
Psyche on the mountaintop. Filled with sorrow, fear, and
dread, she wept inconsolably until she fell asleep. The gentle
west wind, Zephyr (Greek: Zephyrus), soothed her with gentle
breezes.

When she awoke in the morning, Psyche found herself in a

palace grander than any she had ever imagined. Dozens of beautiful servant girls attended her every whim. They placed her in the most comfortable bed wherein she had ever slept. During the night she was gently awakened by the loveliest voice she had ever heard; it was her lover. In the darkness, his skin and body felt like that of a beautiful youth, not a winged monster. She was certain that this was a youth of great beauty, perhaps even a god. After their first night together, she resolved to see his face.

Her lover was insistent, however, that she should never, under any circumstances, look at his face in the light. Once she had seen his face, he warned, he would have to leave her forever. So, she endured this rule for a time, while always pleading for just one glimpse. He consistently refused, which made her curiosity all the more powerful.

One day she coaxed him into allowing her sisters to visit the palace. He was reluctant to do this, but was so madly in love with her that he could not refuse. So, during the day, the gentle wind Zephyr whisked the sisters up to the palace for a visit. The sisters, though married to wealthy men, were unprepared for the opulence they saw and became insanely jealous of Psyche. The visiting sisters began to ask Psyche probing questions about her lover while the three of them feasted on exquisite foods. As she had never seen his face, Psyche's answers were full of inconsistencies.

The sisters quickly noticed the holes in Psyche's stories and began to taunt her by saying, "This is a splendid palace, but that is too high a price to pay for having to sleep with a monster." When the sisters left, Psyche was filled with doubt. On the one hand, she was fairly certain that her lover was a handsome young man. Or did it only seem so? Maybe her sisters had a point: she had never seen his face. Perhaps he *was* a monster.

Psyche now resolved that she would try to see his face by stealth. She stayed up waiting for him to return. When he finally walked into the dark bedroom and fell into a sound sleep, she slipped down the hall and grabbed an oil lamp, which she brought to the bedroom. Seeing him for the first time in the light, she could not believe her eyes: this was the most handsome youth in the world, perhaps even a god. She leaned over to kiss him. Then some of the hot oil spilled from the lamp onto his shoulder, waking him with a start.

He leapt up from the bed and shouted, "I told you *never* to look at my face!" Taking on the divine mantle of invisibility, he fled the room. She raced down the hall after him, but it was too late. As she ran, she heard him identify himself; it was Cupid! And his final words to her that night were that love could not dwell where there is no trust.

Cupid sped to the home of Venus, his mother. He had a rather painful burn on his shoulder where the hot oil had dripped, and he wanted her to tend to it. When he told his mother the story of Psyche, she became enraged. She now hated this beautiful mortal more than ever. The girl had not only been a threat to the cult of Venus, but she had had an affair with Venus's own son!

Psyche knew that she was doomed. Not only was it clear enough that the affair with Cupid was over . . . her very life was now in danger. All that she could do was to throw herself at the feet of Venus, beg for mercy, and vow to serve the goddess all her days. She was hoping that the goddess had at least one ounce of compassion left.

The kindly Zephyr carried Psyche to the chambers of

Venus, who was relishing the chance for revenge on her mortal rival. Psyche flung herself at the feet of the goddess, pleading for mercy. Venus decided to give Psyche an impossible task and then destroy her. So she handed Psyche a pile of the smallest seeds—poppy, millet, and mustard—and ordered her to separate them by kind before nightfall. The task was impossible, and Psyche began to cry. As her tears hit the floor, the little ants took pity on her. The queen ant ordered her subjects to get to work and help Psyche separate the seeds by kind. Soon, with thousands of busy ants working, the job was done. When Venus returned and saw this, she was angrier than before. In fact, the ants have lived underground since that time to avoid her wrath.

As night fell, Psyche became very hungry. But Venus gave her only a morsel of dry bread and forced her to sleep on the cold stone floor. After all, as goddess of beauty, Venus knew that nothing can destroy beauty like privation.

The next day Venus gave Psyche another impossible task: to gather golden fleece. Down in a valley near a river, Venus kept a flock of sacred sheep with golden fleece. However, these sheep had heads like lions and had already torn many mortals to shreds; their bleached bones lay behind, glistening in the sun. Psyche went down to the riverbank and wept, resigned to her doom. Utterly despondent, she contemplated drowning herself in the river. Just then, she heard a sweet little voice, like that of a child. Between her toes was a tiny reed that advised her to pick the golden fleece from the thorny brambles where the sheep had passed through. This way she could gather plenty of the golden wool in safety. Soon Psyche had gathered as much golden wool as she could carry. She had completed Venus's second impossible assignment.

Venus was still prepared to destroy Psyche, so she gave the

girl a pitcher and ordered her to fill it with water from the falls on the River Styx. This river was the border between the lands of the living and the dead. When Psyche arrived, it again appeared that she was in mortal peril. In order to reach the waterfall, she had to climb up slippery rocks alongside boiling rapids that could sweep her down to the land of the dead. Left to her own devices, Psyche would have been finished.

But a great eagle, probably Jupiter (Greek: Zeus) in disguise, took pity on Psyche and swept her safely up to the waterfall. Psyche filled the pitcher to the brim and returned to Venus.

Venus then sent Psyche directly to the land of the dead. Psyche was to ask Proserpina (Greek: Persephone), queen of the underworld, for some of her beauty to replenish Venus, who had begun to show the strain of plotting revenge.

Very few mortals have ever visited the underworld and returned to tell the tale. It is the abode of the dead, and the living cannot return unless they have the help of the gods. Psyche passed a magic tower, where a guide took compassion on her. The guide told her that she would need to pay a fare to Charon, the ferryman of the dead, to take her across the River Styx into the land of the dead. When Psyche responded that she had no money, the guide told her that Charon, grim though he was, was particularly partial to honey cakes; so the guide gave her a cake to give to the ferryman. It is very likely that this guide was the god Mercury (Greek: Hermes), who directs the dead to the underworld, protects travelers, and makes a point of helping lost causes.

Psyche entered the underworld without incident. When she arrived at the throne of Proserpina, the goddess gladly put some of her beauty into a box and sent it along with Psyche.

Now here is where Psyche failed miserably. For however

wise and good a woman may be, she will do anything for the secret of eternal beauty. Psyche held the secret of eternal beauty right in her own hands and the curiosity was killing her. As she walked along, she grew obsessed by the contents of the box. When she opened it, it appeared to be empty. Then she fell into a deep sleep, more beautiful than ever.

Before Venus had time to wonder what was keeping Psyche, Cupid stepped in to save the mortal girl. Forbidden to see Psyche and ordered by his mother to remain in her home, he escaped from the palace of Venus—for not even gods can imprison love. He immediately found Psyche, put some of the beauty back in the box and kissed her, which caused her to wake. Cupid told Psyche to immediately take the box to Venus without fear.

As Psyche started on her way, Cupid went to Jupiter to proclaim his love for Psyche and ask the help of the master of all the gods in uniting them forever.

Jupiter listened sympathetically to Cupid's story and then told the young god, "I don't have to do a thing! Once physical love (eros) and the soul (psyche) are united, not even the gods can separate them. Therefore you and Psyche shall be husband and wife." Jupiter sent for Psyche, and she drank the celestial ambrosia that transforms mortals into immortals. Psyche and Cupid then lived happily among the gods. Venus was so pleased that her former rival was no longer on earth— out of sight of the human beings whose adoration Venus desired—that she actually turned into a rather nice mother-in-law. And so it was that physical love and the soul were united, but only after many difficult trials.

The Last Sighting of Venus: Tannhäuser (Germany)

Medieval Germany, as the following story demonstrates, was a cultural crossroads wherein the classical tradition of Greece and Rome as well as Christianity met with the earlier Germanic traditions. The story of Venus here takes place in a mountain that was believed to be sacred to her Germanic equivalent, Freya. The literate of this time wrote in Latin; the oral poetry of the people, such as the story of Tannhäuser, was sung in German. Thus, the story of Tannhäuser was a German ballad, with a Christian theme featuring a Latin goddess and possibly her Germanic counterpart.

The story of Tannhäuser dates back to the 1200s, when there was a historical minstrel named Tannhäuser. Is it a myth or a legend? It is both, as the thread that is common to both myth and legend is woven throughout and Venus appears much as she did in antiquity. German poet Ludwig Uhland (1787–1862) wrote a poem based on the old tale in suitable Swabian dialect, which we cite here, and which formed the basis of Richard Wagner's opera. For Wagner (1813–1883), the theme of a man's salvation through the love of a good woman was an important romantic theme, not only in his *Tannhäuser*, but also in *Der Fliegende Holländer* (*The Flying Dutchman*).

In Christian times, the gods of antiquity had to flee. Venus took refuge in Hörselberge, or Venusberg, in the German state of Thuringia, near Eisenach. There she was fond of luring handsome young men into her underground lair, where she kept them as her lovers at the price of their eternal souls. By being the lovers of a pagan goddess, they forfeited any chance at Christian salvation. One of these hapless young men was the mastersinger and knight Tannhäuser. With a seductive song and tempting vision, Venus seduced Tannhäuser to spend a year with her as her lover. At the gate of her lair stood the faithful Christian, Eckhardt, who warned of the dangers that awaited those who entered Venusberg.

After a year of sensuous delights, Tannhäuser began to feel remorse and the yearning for Christian salvation. He at first asked Venus politely for permission to leave, but she evaded the question. As he pressed the point, Venus became angry and told him that there was nothing for him in the outside world. If Tannhäuser left her, she warned, he could never hope for forgiveness from the Christian god and would be both despised and pitied by humankind. In despair, Tannhäuser cried out to the Blessed Virgin Mary. The very mention of her name was so powerful that the spell was broken, Venus vanished, and Tannhäuser was at last free to leave. But his problems were hardly over: in order to have his salvation restored, Tannhäuser knew that he had to confess and receive absolution for his great sin.

Upon his return to the upper world, Tannhäuser encountered his friends, including the *Landgraf* (Count) Hermann, master of the Wartburg castle, as well as the Meistersinger (master singers) Wolfram and Walther. They were so overjoyed to see Tannhäuser that they immediately invited him to a feast and song competition in the Wartburg castle. But when they asked Tannhäuser where he had been for the last year, he was evasive and vaguely alluded to travels.

At the castle was the chaste and beautiful Elizabeth (identified with Saint Elizabeth of Hungary). Tannhäuser had loved Elizabeth from afar before his sojourn with Frau Venus, and she had kept a place for him in her heart as well. Wolfram began the song contest by singing romantic songs about how

he had loved Elizabeth from afar. As the Meistersinger kept
singing, Tannhäuser became impatient to have his chance to
sing. Finally, when his turn came, he blurted out what he knew
best: a song from Venusberg (*Dir Göttin der Liebe*—to you, O
goddess of love!)—a hymn to Venus! As good Christians who
were well aware of Venusberg, the entire assembly was shocked!
Hermann angrily ordered Tannhäuser to leave the Wartburg
castle at once, lest he bring a curse on everyone there.

Elizabeth followed Tannhäuser out of the castle and vowed
to pray for his soul. Just as Tannhäuser threw himself at her
feet, the sound of a procession of penitent pilgrims on their
way to Rome could be heard in the distance. Elizabeth told
Tannhäuser that this was his chance to receive absolution and
salvation. Joyously, Tannhäuser joined the throng and made
his way to Rome, leaving Elizabeth in fervent prayer on his
behalf.

Upon arriving in Rome, Tannhäuser threw himself at the
feet of the pope and confessed his sin:

Ach bapst, lieber herre mein!	Oh pope, my dear lord!
Ich klag euch hie mein sünde	I mourn to you my sin
die ich mein tag begangen hab	that I did in a day now passed
als ich euch will verkünden.	and wish to confess.
Ich bin gewesen auch ain jar	I was with Venus the woman
bei Venus einer frawen	for one whole year
nun wolt ich beicht und büβ	and now I wish to repent and
empfahn	be absolved
ob ich möcht Gott anschawen.	and want God to look on me.
Der bapst het ain steblin in	The pope had a staff in his
seiner hand	hand
und as was also durre.	that was absolutely dry and
'Als wenig das steblin	sterile.
gronen mag	"You will be forgiven

Kumstu zu Gottes hulde.'   The day that this staff turns
                                     green!"

                              —Ludwig Uhland, German poet (1787–1862)
                              (Translation, J.F.B.)

In other words, Tannhäuser's sin was so great that the pope
thought it more likely that his staff would sprout green shoots
and blossom than Tannhäuser receive absolution.

Meanwhile, back at the Wartburg castle, Elizabeth eagerly
awaited the return of Tannhäuser. Soon she saw a vast throng
of returned pilgrims singing in joy and religious zeal. As the
band of pilgrims passed by, Elizabeth waited and prayed to
see Tannhäuser. But when Tannhäuser came, he was pale,
miserable, and shaken with grief. Wolfram (in Wagner's version) or Eckhardt (in the medieval version) was shocked to see
Tannhäuser in such a reduced and pathetic state. Wolfram,
confused, asked Tannhäuser whether he had actually made the
trip to Rome, and why did he look so miserable while the other
pilgrims were rejoicing? When Tannhäuser told the story of
his encounter with the pope, Wolfram became very sad.

Then Tannhäuser told Wolfram that if he was damned
anyway, he may as well just go back to live with Venus and
make the rest of his life at least tolerable by immersing himself in sensuous pleasure. Wolfram tried to reason with
Tannhäuser and offered to sit down and talk, but Tannhäuser
told Wolfram not to even sit near him; he was so wretched that
a curse could spill over onto Wolfram.

Hearing Tannhäuser's words, Venus again beckoned him
with a seductive song and appeared to him in a vision, languishing on her couch. Tannhäuser was prepared to return to
her, and Wolfram had to physically restrain him. At last, Wolfram told Tannhäuser that he could not rejoin Venus, because

an angel (Elizabeth) was praying for him. When Tannhäuser
repeated Elizabeth's name, the power of her holiness was so
great that Venus disappeared (in Wagner's version singing
Weh! Mir Verloren!— O Pain, he is lost to me!) with a shriek.

Just as Tannhäuser was regaining his wits, another procession was wending its way to the Wartburg castle—a funeral procession. Elizabeth had died. Tannhäuser then cried out, "Holy
Elizabeth, pray for me!" Tannhäuser followed the procession,
threw himself on the ground at Elizabeth's bier, and died.

Just as Tannhäuser gave his last breath, something wonderful
happened. A pilgrim who had virtually run all the way from
Rome carried the pope's staff—now blossoming with flowers.

Heil! Heil! Die Gnade Wunder Heil!	Hail, Hail, the miracle of grace, Hail!
Erlösung ward der Welt zu Teil.	Redemption has come into the world.
Es tat in nächtlich heil'ger Stund'	It happened during a holy hour in the night.
der Herr sich durch ein Wunder kund.	The Lord has made a miracle.
Den dürren Stab in Priesters hand	The dry staff in the priest's hand
hat er geschmückt mit frischem Grün.	is now adorned with fresh green.
dem Sünder in der Hölle brand	The sinner in the fires of hell
soll so Erlösung neu erblühn.	thus blooms anew through redemption.

—Richard Wagner, *Tannhäuser,* Act III, Scene III
(Translation, J.F.B.)

Tannhäuser, through true penitence and the intercession of
Elizabeth, joined her in heaven.

Heilig die Reine, die nun vereint	Holy, the pure one is united
göttlichen Schar vor dem Ewigen steht.	with the godly host that stand before the Eternal.
Selig der Sünder, dem sie geweint	Blessed is the sinner for whom she wept,
dem die des Himmels erfleht!	her intercession gaining him Heaven.
. . . Der Gnade Heil is dem Büsse bescheiden	. . . Saving grace is imparted to the penitent.
er geht nun ein in der Selig frieden.	He now enters the blessed peace.

Connections

The story of Tannhäuser is a perfect place to end the story of Aphrodite/Venus; she figuratively appears in the story in her three aspects: Venus Urania (the Queen of Heaven, the Blessed Virgin); Venus Genetrix, the loving mother (the faithful—and chaste—lover Elizabeth); and Aphrodite Pornos, the sultry seductress. The orthodox Freudian will see an obvious id (Pornos), ego (Genetrix), and superego (Urania) image here. This corresponds to the three Greek words for *love: eros* (romantic love), *agape* (the selfless love of a mother, for example), and *philos* (friendship or brotherly love).

Aphrodite Pornos, of course, appears in the first myth, "The Infidelity of Aphrodite," where she is the adulterous lover of the hated Ares, god of war. This story is not about romantic love, but pure lust, and is but a guidepost along the way to our understanding of love. Why should there be a union between erotic love and violence? Why should there be a union between Hephaestus, the lame smith of the gods, and Aphrodite? First, the Greeks clearly saw war and lust without love to be manifestations of the baser side of our nature. The result of the union of Ares and Aphrodite—of blood lust and lust—were the twin sons Phobos (fear) and Deimos (dread) and the daughter Harmonia (harmony). The male offspring are, of course, attributes of war. Harmony, the female child, like harmony in music, is the result of counterpoint—in this case, between love and war. If strife were not present, harmony would have no meaning.

The second story, "The Judgment of Paris," is yet another guidepost on the way to romantic love. Discord tosses an apple into a wedding reception—a love feast—beginning an egotistical contest between three vain goddesses. (In Latin, *malum* means both *apple* and *evil*.) Given a choice between invincibility in battle (offered by Athena), mastery of Asia (offered by Hera), or the love of the most beautiful woman (offered by Aphrodite), Paris makes the last of these his choice, as given the choice between power, wealth, and sex, many an impulsive young man would choose the latter.

We finally arrive at romantic love in the story of Cupid and Psyche, wherein Aphrodite Pornos is the villainness, because she is threatened by true romantic love, herein defined as the union of physical love (eros) and the soul (psyche). Despite all of the trials and obstacles that Aphrodite Pornos places in their path, the union of the soul and physical love is invincible.

Tannhäuser is a powerful statement of the power of love to transform. He has "grown up" from the sensuous pleasures offered by Venus Pornos to achieve salvation through the selfless love of Elizabeth. Venus is selfish and manipulative; Tannhäuser feels empty after staying with her. The love that Tannhäuser craves, the love that transforms him, is utterly selfless and giving. Tannhäuser's friends are quick to condemn him upon hearing the forbidden Venusberg song;

Elizabeth is not. The pope withholds absolution from Tannhäuser, believing him beyond redemption; Elizabeth gives her life for his redemption. In Elizabeth's death, the transformed Tannhäuser dies to join her in heaven. Venus's pleasures are temporary; selfless love is eternal. Love is, once again, stronger than death.

AKIKO THE BUTTERFLY
(Japan)

Japanese art, culture, mythology, and folklore all reflect a deep and inherent love of nature. Unlike Westerners, Japanese tend to see themselves as a part of nature rather than distinct from it. One of the most persistent images from nature in Japanese art and literature is the beloved *chocho*, the butterfly whose powers of transformation speak to our own hopes of transformation.

This charming story from Japan is actually a folktale, not a myth. Yet it speaks to the mythic theme of the power of love to transform. In Japan, far removed from Cupid and Psyche, the soul is a butterfly and love transforms.

There was once an old man named Takahama, who lived a very quiet life. Many thought it was strange that, although he had come from a distinguished family and served an apprenticeship for a powerful merchant, he chose the profession of caretaker at a cemetery and lived in the very humble house on the cemetery grounds, amid the tombs. Since he had never married, his sister and her son frequently came to look in on him. It was a trial for them, as it was very eerie to have an uncle who lived in a cemetery; the nephew frequently tried to make excuses to avoid visiting his uncle and always suggested that they invite the uncle to visit them.

One day his sister and nephew went to see him and found him mortally ill. As old Takahama fell asleep, a little white butterfly flew around the old man's face and rested on the pillow. The nephew was annoyed and three times tried to shoo it away; still the butterfly appeared determined to be near old Takahama. When Takahama drew his last breath, the butterfly flew out of the house. Knowing that this might be an omen, the nephew followed the butterfly, which flew to the grave of a young woman named Akiko and then disappeared. The grave of Akiko was old and covered with moss. This Akiko had died some sixty years earlier, but still there were fresh, recently watered flowers by the grave. Seldom does one see such things on such an old tomb.

The nephew came back and told his mother what had happened. The mother closed her eyes and smiled knowingly. "What was the name on the grave?" she asked. When the son said, "Akiko," she told this story.

"Many years ago old Takahama was hopelessly in love with a beautiful girl named Akiko, and they became engaged, but she died before the wedding day. Takahama could not bear to be separated from her and left his promising career to always be near her. Every day, whether he was ill or well, and regardless of the weather, Takahama would tend to her grave. In the spring, summer, and autumn, he always brought fresh flowers; in winter, he placed evergreen boughs on her tomb. This must be the first day that he has missed tending to her tomb in over sixty years! That little butterfly was her soul. She probably was concerned when Takahama didn't show up today and decided that she should look in on him. And she didn't leave until his soul left to be with her."

Connections

The crux of this story is *selfless* love is stronger than death. Love defines Takahama in death as in life. Like Paris and Aphrodite, Takahama chooses love over wealth and power, but it is a selfless love, not lust. As he is faithful to Akiko in life, so she is faithful to him in death.

THE WOOING OF ETAIN
(Ireland)

It is seldom remembered that Irish literature is the third oldest written literature in Europe to come to us intact, surpassed only by Latin and Greek. Irish mythology is very much concerned with issues of romantic love, and the women in Irish myths, such as this one and the one that follows, are strong, assertive, and powerful.

This is another love–as–butterfly story, only from Ireland. This myth shares the theme of Nala and Damayanti: that when a woman is given the choice between marrying a god and a mortal, she will choose the mortal.

Midir the Proud was the son of the Dagda, the king of the gods, and took as his second wife a young half-mortal beauty named Etain. Not surprisingly, his first wife Fuamnach grew very jealous and used magic to change Etain into a butterfly, and then conjured up strong winds to blow Etain out of the palace and toss her the length and breadth of Ireland for seven years. One day by chance a gentle breeze blew the little butterfly through a window in the palace of Angus, the god of love.

A curious thing then happened. The divine Angus immediately recognized Etain as immortal and, although unable to undo Fuamnach's spell, decided to make her as happy and comfortable as possible. He built her a garden and stocked it with every kind of flower that butterflies love. Etain flittered happily in the sunlight by day. However, when the little flowers closed up in the evening, Etain regained her human form and she and Angus became lovers. Some say it was the love of Angus that allowed this transformation to take place.

But Fuamnach had sources throughout the country, and she learned of Etain's happy life with Angus. Her jealousy had not lessened in the seven years, and so she again summoned the winds. This time they blew Etain far from Angus, all the way to the court of Etar in Ulster. Etain landed in the drinking cup of Etar's wife, who swallowed her, became pregnant, and gave birth to a baby, whom she named Etain.

Etain grew into a very beautiful girl, and it happened that Eochy, the *Ard-Ri* (High King) of All Ireland, was in search of a wife. He asked the nobles to find him a suitable and beautiful consort, for there was to be an assembly of all the noble houses of Ireland, and if only Eochy arrived unescorted, there would be a serious breach of protocol. Eochy took one look at Etain and fell hopelessly in love, and the two were married.

King Eochy had a brother named Ailill who also fell hopelessly in love with Etain, to the point that it made him deathly ill. Eochy was called away from his capital at Tara on some urgent state business and left Etain to care for his ailing brother. Etain patiently nursed him, but Ailill did not improve. Finally, she asked him the cause of his illness. He hedged at first, saying, "It is closer to me than my skin; it is like fighting a spirit; it is like a treasure unobtainable hidden beneath the sea; it is a passion for an echo." Etain at first thought that

Ailill was delirious from fever. Then Ailill burst out that he was dying of being in love with her.

Now Etain had a great dilemma. If Ailill died while Eochy was away, her husband would be stricken with grief. If, however, she made love to Ailill, she would be unfaithful—another unacceptable alternative. She decided that perhaps the best way for her to be faithful to Eochy was to be unfaithful to him. It would not do for her to sleep with Ailill in Eochy's own palace, so she arranged an assignation at a nearby house.

Etain went to the house, but Ailill never showed up. A spirit in the form of Ailill went to the house but behaved very oddly, merely stating the cause of Ailill's illness and abruptly leaving. The real Ailill never left the palace, having fallen into a deep sleep, from which he awoke with his desire for Etain completely gone. Now poor Etain was even more confused.

The spirit who had appeared to Etain was her original husband in her previous life, Midir the Proud, whom she did not recognize.

Knowing that Etain had been completely baffled, the stranger (Midir) returned the next day dressed in his finest clothing. He explained that it was he who caused Ailill to fall into a deep sleep. Moreover, Fuamnach, who had previously tormented her, was now dead. He then begged her to return with him to the Tir Na Og (the Land of Youth), lyrically telling of its wonders.

Etain tried to find a way out of this; she agreed to go with Midir, providing that her husband consented! When Eochy returned, Midir set out on a strategy that would result in his obtaining Etain.

Midir challenged Eochy to a game of chess on a board of

silver with pieces made of gold and jewels. Midir let Eochy win game after game, and as payment for his gambling losses, Midir increased Eochy's harvests, drained swamps, and generally improved the land. One day, at last, Midir defeated Eochy. As Midir had been scrupulous in paying his gambling debts, Eochy was now prepared to honor his. Eochy offered Midir anything in his kingdom as payment.

"Etain," replied Midir.

Stunned, Eochy sat back, pursed his lips, and remained silent for what seemed like hours. Then he said, "Come back in one month and collect your winnings."

Human beings are fools; they have never learned that they cannot outsmart the gods. Kings, with all their power, are the slowest to grasp this. Over the next month Eochy, being no exception, surrounded his palace with a host of armed warriors to prevent Midir from taking Etain. Thinking himself safe in the palace, Eochy set about drinking and feasting with his court. Just as Etain passed the wine, the divine Midir appeared in their midst with a spear in one hand, put the other arm around Etain, and flew out with her through a palace window.

Eochy went into a rage and began digging up the *side*, the sacred mounds where the gods can be found. Having been defeated by the supernatural, Eochy sought the help of a druid named Dalan. As wise as Dalan was, he tried for one year to come up with a means to retrieve Etain, but nothing worked.

Dalan then turned to divination using three bunches of yew branches, whereupon words were written in the sacred ogham script. Dalan located Etain at the sacred mound of Brilleath. Eochy spent nine years digging up mounds throughout

Ireland, which Midir magically filled as quickly as they were dug. At last Eochy found the correct mound and recovered Etain.

Midir again attempted to fool the king into losing Etain. He sent fifty servant girls, all of whom were identical to Etain. It was virtually impossible to distinguish the false Etain from the real. But the eyes of love see differently, and Eochy noticed that one of the girls poured wine in the manner that only Etain used to do. However, this woman, as much as she looked like Etain, was still not the same person as his wife.

The name of this woman actually was Etain—it was Etain and Eochy's daughter, the very image of her mother. Midir explained that Etain was pregnant with the baby when he took Etain away.

The mother Etain, who had quietly watched the scene from an alcove, appeared and ran to embrace Eochy. Given the choice between a man and a god, a woman will choose a man.

The younger Etain married King Cormac, and her grandson, in turn, was Conaire Mor, greatest of the High Kings of Ireland.

Connections

Etain, through a curse, becomes a butterfly, but is transformed at night into Angus's lover, through the "magic" of the love of Angus. Love breaks the curse, as it did for Nala and Damayanti. And Eochy, after many trials and defying even the trickery of the gods, is defeated, only to finally win Etain. Once again, a woman (even if only half mortal) chooses a mortal over a god.

Indeed, Ailill's declaration of love for Etain is a timeless statement of unrequited love: "It is closer to me than my skin;

it is like fighting a spirit; it is like a treasure unobtainable hidden beneath the sea; it is a passion for an echo."

Another important parallel exists between the story of Etain and that of Nala and Damayanti, in that the gods try to deceive the humans by making many physically identical Nalas or Etains, but the lover alone can identify the true one by seeing that "certain something" that only lovers see. Love is stronger than magic; it cannot be deceived, and no trial can defeat it.

THE ONLY JEALOUSY OF EMER
(Ireland)

This myth introduces us to the Irish cultural hero, Cuchulain, and his wife, Emer. Emer herself is a formidable warrior. Unlike the myths of many other traditional cultures, the Irish myths often feature women leading troops into battle, even taking part in one-on-one sword and spear battles against the males. Such a woman does not easily accept the unfaithfulness of her husband.

The story so captivated the Irish poet and playwright William Butler Yeats that he wrote a successful play based on it. Love is put to the test as spouses are unfaithful, but the unfaithful lovers each know that the love of even the wronged spouse has a redeeming power.

Cuchulain was the greatest hero of the Irish. Once, he was tired from hunting and lay resting against a pillar stone, when he fell into a very deep sleep. In his dreams, there appeared two very beautiful maidens armed with rods; they proceeded to beat him with these rods until he was barely alive. When he awoke, he knew that it was more than a dream, as he was in great pain and a wasting sickness set upon him. This pain lasted for an entire year until a stranger appeared one day.

The stranger told Cuchulain to return to the pillar where the vision had occurred and he would at last find relief from his great torment. Upon arriving at this site, Cuchulain saw a beautiful woman dressed in green, whom he recognized as one of the two tormentors in his dream. She informed Cuchulain that she was a messenger sent by Fand, the wife of the sea god Manannan, who had fallen deeply in love with the hero and had been quarreling with her own husband. Fand was now under constant attack by three demon kings from whom only Cuchulain could deliver her.

Suspicious of the story and of Fand's motives, Cuchulain sent Laeg, his chariot driver, to investigate. Laeg went over into the Land of Spirits after crossing a sacred lake in an enchanted boat of bronze. Laeg returned to Cuchulain with stories not only of the incomparable beauty of Fand and her attendants, but also of the many pleasures to be found in abundance in the Land of Spirits. The restless hero rushed to meet Fand, but first had to do battle with the three demon kings, who appeared as sea waves, as they were no doubt under orders from their master and Fand's husband, the sea god Manannan.

Having vanquished the three demons, Cuchulain and Fand became lovers and the hero remained with her for an entire month. Word spread quickly that the two were openly living together, as both of them were married to others. When Cuchulain and Fand needed to part, they pledged to meet for trysts in the future on the bank of a certain river beneath a yew tree. More than a few people overheard this pledge, and word got back to Emer, Cuchulain's wife.

Emer wasn't the jealous type. As a warrior hero, Cuchulain had had many lovers, including Aife, by whom he had already had a child. Emer had taken these in stride as either mere trysts or diversions from war. This time, however, she would not indulge her husband; for Cuchulain to live openly with the very wife of the sea god was more than she could bear. She led fifty of her warrior maidens in chariots on the bank of the trysting place to kill Fand. Emer herself was at the head of the army, her own sword flashing.

Cuchulain saw the chariots approach in the distance and stepped forward to place himself between the army and Fand. The last thing that Emer's horde wished to do was to kill Cuchulain, so they halted.

Seeing this, Cuchulain addressed Emer directly. He spoke of Fand's charm, beauty, and the pleasure that she had brought him.

Emer heard this and replied, rather calmly, "Fand is in no way better than I am. Cuchulain, you know that what is new is always sweet and what is old always seems to have lost its savor. We've been happy before and we could be again, if you would truly love me again."

To which Cuchulain, like many unfaithful husbands, protested by saying that he did indeed love Emer and the affair had been a mistake.

Fand, feeling hurt and used now, addressed them both. "If you feel that way, Cuchulain, then give me up."

Emer proudly responded, "No, my husband was unfaithful to me. He left me for you. If that's what you both want, I will be the one to leave."

The old bards say that Fand took her leave of this tense scene by saying the following:

> Emer, the man is yours
> and may you enjoy him good woman.
> What my hand cannot obtain
> I must still desire.

—Jeffrey Gantz, *Early Irish Myths and Sagas*

So Emer disbanded her armies and went home with her husband. Fand returned to Manannan as well, but was afraid of his reaction to her infidelity. Manannan knew of the shame and grief that Fand felt, and even though her adultery had humiliated him, he still loved her greatly. The sea god looked at Fand with tears in his eyes and asked, "Do you wish to stay with me or go off with Cuchulain?" Fand responded, "Neither of you is better than the other. Cuchulain has Emer, and you have no one but me." So Fand rejoined her husband. As a precaution, however, Manannan put his magic cloak between Fand and Cuchulain so that they would never meet again.

Connections

The torments that Cuchulain suffers are the torments of a conflicted man. He endures much to "win" Fand, only to find that the love is illusory. The women beating him with rods and the battle with the demon kings may signify his struggle with his own conscience.

When Emer decides to bring her army to the trysting place, she is prepared to do battle. But there is no battle. Cuchulain and Fand each know where they belong, and each returns to their spouse. Lust is an illusion that true love can easily shatter.

TRISTAN AND ISOLDE
(Medieval Western Europe)

Tristan and Isolde, like Tannhäuser, is a characteristic romance of the Middle Ages, spread far and wide by ballad singers. This tale, which Richard Wagner presented in operatic form, can be found in medieval references in Britain, France, Italy, Spain, and Germany. Considering the limits of medieval travel and communications, the story must have had great power for the listener in order to both spread and endure.

The tragic, fated love in Tristan and Isolde is a retelling of the ancient story we find in the myth of Pyramus and Thisbe, then Romeo and Juliet, of "star-crossed lovers." The question of whether Tristan and Isolde is truly a myth may be raised, as this is a medieval story with ancient roots that pervade the myths. It has survived because it bears a message as strong as any in the myths. This story contains elements of romantic myths, as well as those of myths of the hero.

Riwalin, king of Parmenia, traveled to Cornwall to visit his ally, King Mark. King Mark's sister Blanchefleur was extremely beautiful, and Riwalin fell hopelessly in love with her. As Parmenia was not as impressive a realm as Cornwall, the couple weren't exactly sure just how well Mark would take to the idea of Riwalin as a brother-in-law, so the two eloped to Parmenia. Unfortunately, shortly thereafter Riwalin was killed in battle. The grief Blanchefleur felt caused her to die while giving birth to their son, Tristan.

Tristan was raised by Riwalin's faithful friend Rual, who treated him as his own dear son. And Tristan was quite a prodigy: by the age of fourteen, he had mastered languages and the arts of chivalry. Entrusting the kingdom of Parmenia to Rual, Tristan set out in search of adventure and ended up in Cornwall, where his uncle, King Mark, still reigned. Tristan did not identify himself immediately as Mark's nephew. Instead, the young stranger astonished the Cornish court with his prodigy and good looks, and soon he had the ear of King Mark himself. Rual appeared in Cornwall after a four-year search for Tristan and told the whole story of Tristan's birth. Accordingly, King Mark hailed the young prodigy as his nephew and made Tristan the heir to the kingdom.

Soon Cornwall, once a proud and independent kingdom, was subjected to the tyranny of Gurmun, king of Ireland, who demanded a horrible tribute of one-third of the wealth of the kingdom. The enforcer and collector of the tribute was Gurmun's cruel brother-in-law, Morold, who was so powerful and fierce that none in Cornwall dared do battle with him—no one, until Tristan appeared on the scene.

Tristan and Morold battled on a small island in the Irish Sea between Cornwall and Ireland. Tristan swiftly dispatched Morold with his sword. The dying Morold had inflicted a major wound on Tristan and warned the Cornish champion that the only person who could heal such a wound was his sister, the queen of Ireland, who had magic powers. After Tristan left the scene, the queen of Ireland arrived and removed a shard of Tristan's sword from the body of her dead brother as a memento.

Tristan returned to Cornwall, but knew that with his wound he did not have much time to figure a way to slip into Ireland unnoticed. Calling himself Tantris, a *Spielmann* (storyteller or bard), he went to Dublin, where he dazzled all and was soon a favorite of the Irish court, including the queen and the beautiful princess, the blond Isolde. The queen quickly hired him to teach Isolde languages, music, and other arts. Isolde fell deeper and deeper in love with him. As it was noticed that Tantris was suffering from a wound, the Irish queen quickly healed it for her friend and benefactor. Tristan then concocted a tale of how he had to return home to look after his adoring wife, which disappointed Isolde mightily, but nonetheless allowed Tristan to return to Cornwall, where King Mark anxiously awaited his heir's return.

Tristan's return to Cornwall delighted King Mark, but annoyed the other nobles, who were jealous of him. Some of the nobles suggested that King Mark marry and produce his own heir (thus depriving Tristan of the throne). Tristan was summoned to King Mark, wherein Tristan sang of the beauty of the young Isolde. To Tristan's disappointment, Mark announced that Isolde would be his own bride. Mark dispatched Tristan to Ireland as his envoy to carry the news. Relations between Cornwall and Ireland had improved; the Irish now respected the Cornish ruler, and commerce had ensued. A marriage of the Irish and Cornish royal houses would be a political benefit to both.

Tristan arrived in Ireland to convey Mark's message. However, Isolde and her mother both recognized Tantris and confronted him with his lies. Worse still, the Irish knew that King Mark's nephew, one Tristan, was the killer of Morold. Isolde's love turned into hate when she examined the shard left in Morold's body; it so happened that a chunk the very size and shape of the shard was missing from Tristan's blade! And what of this lie about the "adoring wife" back home? Isolde now loathed Tristan.

But the Irish queen, despite her contempt for Tristan, knew of the immense political advantages of a marriage between Isolde and Mark. The trade between Cornwall and Ireland was profitable and more economically advantageous than exacting tribute. Ireland had other enemies and could use an alliance with Cornwall. So the queen agreed to send Isolde to Cornwall to marry Mark. But Mark was getting old and Isolde was young and beautiful; the queen could not afford to have Isolde trapped in a loveless marriage. So, using her considerable skills, the queen concocted a love potion that would create great passion between the two.

Isolde boarded the ship, sulking because she could hardly stand the sight of Tristan. Her attendant, Brigäne, however, knew that it was essential to reconcile Tristan and Isolde. She explained to Isolde that despite his killing Morold, his posing as Tantris, and his chronic mendacity, Tristan was still the same man who had been Isolde's tutor. And after all, he was merely doing his patriotic duty in killing Morold. Isolde and Tristan, explained Brigäne, had to be friends in order to make Isolde have a happy life in Cornwall. Certainly Tristan would apologize.

Soon Brigäne brought Tristan and Isolde together and they patched things up, deciding to drink to their new friendship. Now, some say that Brigäne purposely did this and others say it was an honest accident, but Brigäne made a most tragic slipup; she confused the bottle of love potion with a bottle of wine! Tristan and Isolde drank the potion, were seized with passion for each other, and immediately made love. The potion was so strong that all shame, guilt, honor, and propriety dissolved. Then again, maybe the potion merely accentuated the feelings that were already there. Then again, maybe the drink *was* just wine, and the two had acted on existing feelings. Regardless, it certainly created a problem for the bride of King Mark.

Upon their arrival in Cornwall, Isolde married Mark; however, Isolde could not spend the wedding night with Mark without his discovery that she was not a virgin, so Brigäne went to bed with Mark in place of Isolde, undetected. The web of deceit and falsehood grew greater and greater, as Tristan and Isolde slipped away many times to continue their passionate affair. It wasn't long before rumors were whispered at court, and Isolde volunteered to undergo a test of truth.

She said she would swear an oath of faithfulness to King Mark and then volunteer to hold a red-hot iron. If she lied, she would be badly burned; if she told the truth, she would be unharmed. Now, the oath ended up being vague: Isolde swore that she had never slept with anyone but one who was born to the throne of Cornwall—an apt description for Tristan as much as Mark. There were plenty of other loopholes, and Isolde escaped unharmed, to the satisfaction of Mark but no one else in the Cornish court.

The nobles had urged King Mark to marry in order to produce an heir to supplant Tristan's claim to the throne, but after months of marriage, Isolde was not pregnant. The king and his nobles went hunting one day and returned to find Tristan and Isolde in flagrante delicto on the king's very bed! That was more than Mark could bear. He cried out, "How could you, my nephew and heir, repay my kindness, my love, and my trust in such a manner?" And then he turned to Isolde, shouting, "Adulteress! Go back to Ireland whence you came." Then Mark banished them both from his kingdom.

Tristan wandered off to the court of the duke of Arundel, where he once more gained favor and met a woman also named Isolde, but Isolde of the White Hands was a brunette, unlike his blond true love. Tristan had thoughts only for the blond Isolde, but he also yearned to explain things to King Mark and resume his role as heir to the throne. Tristan and brunette Isolde boldly went to Cornwall, where he was wounded by a poison lance thrust at him by his own uncle Mark. He retired to a castle to die, some say on an island off Cornwall. He told the second Isolde that he could be healed by the magic touch of the first Isolde, and a faithful servant went to Ireland to fetch the first Isolde. Now, if the returning ship carried the blond Isolde, it would have a white sail; if not, a black sail (the same code appears in the Greek myth of Theseus). Tristan was so ill that he could not lift himself from his bed. He asked the second Isolde whether the returning sail was white or black. The ship actually had a white sail, but the jealous wife lied and told Tristan that the sail was black; she would rather lose him to death than to the arms of another woman. Thereupon, Tristan fell dead.

The blond Isolde arrived on the scene to find Tristan dead, and she herself fell dead.

Brigäne went to King Mark and explained how she had confused the wine with the love potion and that neither Tristan nor Isolde could help their passion for each other. Mark forgave them then and had the lovers buried next to each other, planting a white rose bush on each grave (some say a lily); in time, the two bushes grew so intertwined that they appeared to be one bush. If anyone eats from this bush (shades of the Garden of Eden), they are seized with either passion or fertility.

(Note: The opera lovers among us will say, "But that isn't how the story goes!" The above telling of the story is based upon the Tristan of German poet Gottfried von Strassburg [about 1210], and thence from Ludwig Uhland's translation into modern German. There are some key differences from the Wagner opera, but the plot is essentially the same.)

Connections

What was in the cup? Was it really an irresistible love potion or merely wine? Did it awaken feelings that were already there?

This story is about love as transformation. The Tristan we meet at the beginning of the story is charming, handsome, clever, and deceitful. The Tristan we meet at the end is not the Tristan of the beginning of the story; this is now a man who has faced great trials, lost a throne and his reputation, and who now lies dying. Only the sight of his true love can save him. Love in this tale is even stronger than the knowledge that Tristan has murdered Isolde's uncle. And once again, love is stronger than death, as two little flower bushes grow on the dead lovers' graves and become so entwined that they become one bush.

The myths of love speak to us by addressing the six critical elements of the human condition. They address human *finitude* in that there are clear distinctions between gods and mortals, the latter defined by the certainty of death. More powerfully, these myths speak to our process of *becoming*, as love has the power to transform. In these myths, critical *choices* are made that, as often as not, have great costs. But the most important element addressed in these myths is that we are social beings, and our *existence is with, in, and through others*. Lovers are those who enter our existence and alter it forever.

The next chapter is concerned with our *identity and participation* in the cosmos, and our inherent estrangement. Our considerations of romantic love have provided many insights into human nature, and the symbolism of love that comes from nature is in the form of butterfly, swan, and flower. The themes of nature and human nature, as well as that of love as stronger than death, accompany us into a consideration of myths that are, on one level, an explanation of natural phenomena—and on a deeper level, a consideration of who we are in the cosmos, and in the cycle of life and death.

3. Myths of Nature and Human Nature

In this chapter, we see a mythic worldview doing what it does best: explaining the neverending cycles of birth, death, and rebirth. But, it also explains our place in that cycle. In the mythic worldview, there is little distinction between the human and the plant cycle of death and rebirth. There is no linear history, but an endless replaying of a cycle of life and death that is common to all creatures. Yet, the question of what happens to us when we die finds only a limited answer in the analogy of the seed that dies in the ground and sprouts up in the springtime. So these myths also say something about meaning.

Myths of nature and human nature are a response to the perennial questions of human finitude and our place in the cosmos. They typically represent a worldview where humankind is not separate from nature, but rather express that as the human is part of nature, so is nature part of the human. Still, they do not imply that we have no more meaning than any other living creature, for one difference between humans and nature is humankind's ability to communicate. Human beings in the myths go to the place of the dead and report back on what they have seen. This is a great potential source of meaning, as there are reports from travelers between the two worlds of the dead and the living who return to tell us that our finitude is illusory and that death is a passage and not the end.

THE MYTH OF KORE (PERSEPHONE)
(Greece)

This myth is considered one of the culturally most important of the Greek myths. It was the basis of an important body of religious faith and ritual that was used to comfort the bereaved at funerals, and is believed to be a version of one of the most ancient of all stories, with roots in Mesopotamia and Egypt.

Demeter (Roman: Ceres [barley mother]) is the goddess of agriculture and was considered one of the founders of civilization. The Roman poet Ovid (in Book V of *Metamorphoses*) wrote:

> Ceres was the first to break up the sods of earth with the crooked plough; she first planted corn and cultivated crops; she imposed the first laws on the world. All we have, we owe to Ceres. Of her I must sing: I pray that my songs may be worthy of the goddess, for surely the goddess is worthy of my song.

Demeter bore a daughter by Zeus (Roman: Jupiter) and named her Kore (maiden), who was later known as Persephone (Roman: Proserpina). While Demeter is the patroness of agriculture in all of its forms, Kore is the power of growth that exists in all life, both plant and animal. As Kore grew into womanhood, she became so beautiful that Hades, lord of the underworld, fell hopelessly in love with her. Hades called upon his brother Zeus to seek consent for Kore's hand in marriage.

If Zeus were to consent to Hades' request, he would anger Demeter, who did not wish to be parted from her daughter, let alone send Kore, who represented growth, to live in the gloomy underworld, a place of death and sadness. Were he to deny the request, he would incur the wrath of his own brother and lord of the underworld. And if Hades were angered, Hades easily could have refused to accept the spirits of the dead, who then would end up roaming the surface world, which would create havoc. So, being a well-seasoned diplomat, Zeus talked and talked, without giving or withholding consent.

One day Kore happened to be picking poppies in a field near Eleusis when a great chasm opened in the earth with a thundering sound. Out came Hades driving his chariot of black horses. In one swoop, he grabbed Kore and carried her off to the underworld.

It wasn't long before Demeter began to worry about her daughter's absence. Overcome by grief, she thought of nothing but finding Kore. After ten days of fruitless searching, she came to the home of King Keleus and his wife Metaneira in Eleusis. Demeter hadn't eaten, so they offered food, which the goddess rejected. However, they also offered her the drink that is sacred to her: barley water seasoned with mint. This she gladly accepted.

Demeter explained the cause of her great distress as the entire court listened. One of the king's sons, Triptolemus, then reported a strange story that he had heard from his brothers. The brothers were out in the fields tending to their sheep and pigs when the earth suddenly opened up and swallowed the livestock. In just the twinkling of an eye, the brothers caught a glimpse of a chariot drawn by black horses careening down into the underworld. Most important, they saw that the driver was clutching a young girl and that her cries pierced the air until she vanished beneath the earth.

Armed with this information, Demeter investigated further and went to Helios (Roman: Sol), the sun god, who sees all things. At first, Helios was reluctant to discuss the matter, but where there is light, nothing can be hidden for long—so Helios admitted that Hades had abducted Kore. Since nothing under the sun could take place without Zeus's knowledge, if not his consent, Demeter was livid.

As Demeter was consumed with sorrow, worry, and anger, she forgot to attend to her duties. Every living plant on the earth began to wither and die; soon livestock began perishing by the herd. People had emptied the granaries, and without a new harvest, many began to starve.

All of the gods witnessed this with great concern and pleaded with Zeus to do something; after all, if humankind perished as a result, who would exist to provide sacrifices? What was the point of being a god over a dead universe? Zeus sent his beautiful daughter, Iris the rainbow, to plead with Demeter to return to her duties. The goddess ignored Iris and things continued to worsen. A number of the gods, with the notable exception of Zeus, brought gifts to Demeter in hopes of appeasement, but to no avail. Soon Demeter's mother, Rhea, Mother Earth herself, became desperately ill.

At the same time, Zeus had sent Hermes (Roman: Mercury), messenger of the gods, to negotiate with Hades. What

Zeus and Hades both knew, of course, was that Kore was free to leave as long as she had not eaten the food of the underworld. Since it appeared that Kore hadn't eaten during her sojourn in Hades' realm, there was nothing that compelled Hades to keep her there, other than ego and lust. Hermes pointed out that if Rhea, Mother Earth, died, there would be nothing left alive for the gods to rule. Hades was unconcerned, as he was ruler of the dead. Then Hermes reminded Hades that he was lord of all the riches that lay in the earth—gold, silver, diamonds—hence Hades' other name, Pluto (the rich one). If these riches were not prized by mortals, they would lose their value and Hades would lose much of his prestige. This argument worked until an old gardener burst out that he had seen Kore eat part of a pomegranate, consigning her to life in the underworld.

Hermes' negotiating skills, however, proved adequate to the situation. Kore had not eaten the *whole* pomegranate, just a little bite. Therefore, Kore should be allowed to spend half the year with her mother and the rest in the underworld with Hades. Kore's name was then changed to Persephone (bearer of destruction).

Thus, since that time, the growing season lasts for about half the year, while Persephone is on the surface of the earth with her mother. During the rest of the year when Persephone must reside in the underworld, it is winter and the land remains fallow as Demeter grieves for her daughter and does not allow the earth to produce food. Still apprehensive of Demeter's anger, Helios tries to avert his sun chariot to avoid Demeter during this season, so the days are short and the earth is cold.

The people of Greece never forgot this story and celebrated the Eleusinian Mysteries in honor of Persephone and Demeter in the town of Eleusis, where Demeter was entertained by King Keleus. Indeed, Demeter had rewarded Prince Triptolemus for his assistance in finding her daughter, with the gift of the plow and knowledge of the proper cultivation of grain. In the feast of Thesmophoria, in late September or early October, which is during the harvest and frost season, the people arrived at Eleusis to say farewell to Persephone. In a feast called the Lesser Eleusinia, in February, which is the end of winter in Greece, they met to welcome Kore back to the surface world.

Connections

The story of Kore, or Persephone, has three levels to be considered here: (1) It is a nature myth; (2) it is about human nature; and (3) it is a history of prehistory—a retelling of events before recorded history that give us insight into the most ancient societies.

As a nature myth, the story appears to be a straightforward explanation of the origin of the seasons, particularly with respect to the growing season. The coming of the fall frost in Greece appears to kill the grapevines and olive trees; the growing season ends, and the accompanying rains were called Demeter's tears. But also, it is to the land where the souls of the *human* dead dwell that Kore is abducted and then must spend half the year. There is a connection, thus, between the death of the crops and human death.

The story is set in Eleusis in Greece, where the Eleusinian Mysteries were held to remember the story of Kore and Demeter. The mysteries were a powerful religious retreat wherein the focus of thought and meditation was on rebirth (at one point in history) and resurrection (at another).

It is believed that a discourse was held wherein a barley stalk was held up that appeared dead, with the instruction that just as this stalk bore the seeds of next year's crop, so within our own death there is life. (Note: The same view was expressed by Saint Paul in his first letter to the Corinthians: "That which you sow does not sprout grain unless it dies." [1 Corinthians 15:36])

As a myth of both nature and human nature, this narrative reflects a traditional worldview that did not make a sharp distinction between human life and that of the rest of nature. The ancients perceived themselves as a part of nature; we perceive ourselves today as apart from nature. But the myth also functions as a myth of human nature. The Kore narrative speaks to two of the key elements of the human condition: *it places us in the cosmos* as part of an endless cycle of death and rebirth in order to speak to the anxiety that humans feel when faced with their *finitude*—death. In terms of these elements, the ancients saw an answer to the question of human mortality in observing the endless cycle of death and resurrection in the vegetal world. It is instructive that the crops wither and die when Kore goes to the land of the human dead, as there is but one life force common to both. And even as the cycle of plant death in autumn and winter would be followed by the "resurrection" of plant life in the spring, so, too, was humankind expected to blossom anew. We, however, are alone in the cosmos in that we alone (to the best of our knowledge) can communicate our knowledge of our place in the cosmos as death and rebirth to those after our death; this in itself is a form of immortality.

The myth was also interpreted by Johann Jakob Bachofen (and later, Robert Graves) to be a "history of prehistory," a distant memory of a struggle between a matriarchal society and a patriarchal challenge to this authority, transmitted orally through the myths for centuries. In their view, Demeter was symbolic of a peaceful agricultural society dominated by women, and Hades' seizure of Kore was a sign of a violent, warlike action of males to usurp the existing order. In Bachofen's view, the society was destabilized by a hetairic transition, wherein neither males nor females were dominant, and abduction and rape took the place of marriage. Thus, Hades is violent in seizing Kore, and the mother weeps. Demeter is credited with the establishment of law and culture, which Hades defies. The matriarchal period was characterized by worship of a goddess or goddesses, who in turn were usurped by gods as patriarchy became ascendant. Kore is renamed Persephone, bearer of destruction, not merely as the harbinger of the end of the growing season, but also as harbinger of the death of a stable society.

THE STORY OF SATI
(India)

We noted earlier, in the love story of Nala and Damayanti, that Indian mythology reflects the encounter of two peoples, representing the Indo–Aryan Eurasian myth–producing sphere and the Dravidians of the southern myth–producing area. This myth speaks directly to that encounter. The Hindu god Shiva appears to be of northern origin. His nemesis and father-in-law, Daksha, has a name related to the word for *south*.

Another important cultural note is the power and right of Indian royal princesses to choose their own husbands despite the wishes of their fathers. So many of the myths we have seen are strongly patriarchal, with women in the background. Princess Sati, on the other hand, is a strong–willed woman who knows what she wants and gets it. The source for this story is the Indian national epic, the *Mahabharata*.

Daksha was one of the *Prajapatis*, the rulers chosen by Brahma the Creator to govern the earth. Daksha had twenty-seven daughters, corresponding to the twenty-seven phases of the moon, and all these daughters but the youngest, who was named Sati, were married to the moon god, Soma.

At one point the easily agitated Daksha felt that Soma was paying too much attention to one of the wives, Rohini, at the expense of the others. So Daksha cursed Soma to die of consumption. However, the twenty-seven women pleaded with their father, and so Soma's bouts of consumption became only periodic, corresponding with the waning moon.

Daksha proved to be an equally difficult father when his daughter Sati wanted to marry Shiva, god of destruction. Sati had caught a glimpse of Shiva while still a little girl and fallen instantly in love with him. Unfortunately, the ever contentious Daksha loathed Shiva, because at one time Daksha had hosted a festival and Shiva failed to observe the usual courtesies toward his host. As a result, Daksha denied Shiva any share of the offerings and cursed the god.

Yet one of the privileges of being a princess is to hold a *swayamvara*, an event where an array of suitors is presented to a princess for her to choose from; by custom, the father has no option but to accept her choice. At Sati's *swayamvara*, a parade of handsome, powerful, and rich gods and princes vied for Sati's hand in marriage, but she was bored with all of them, thinking only of Shiva.

It is the custom at a *swayamvara* for the princess to place a wreath of flowers around the neck of her chosen suitor. So Sati threw her wreath into the air, declaring that Shiva was her only love. Upon hearing his name, Shiva appeared and the wreath went around his neck. Daksha was livid, but had no choice but to accept his daughter's choice. Still, Daksha was in no way inclined to make things easy for the couple in the future.

Shiva took Sati to his home in Kailas, beyond the Himalayas (the distance provided one more thing for Daksha to complain about), where Sati and Shiva were adored by *rishis* (holy men) and all sorts of gods and spirits. However, the ascetic side of Shiva soon came out, and he and Sati would dress like beggars and meditate in the mountains.

Daksha wanted to let his son-in-law know of his displeasure at his daughter's lowly estate and willfulness, so he invited all of the gods (except Shiva, of course) to a great festival centered around the sacrifice of a horse. It wasn't long before Sati and Shiva heard about the big event. Sati told Shiva that they should attend, invited or not, just to make a point. Shiva advised against it, as such an episode would only make matters worse. Sati, ever willful, declared that she would go by herself; her father could not turn his own daughter away for any reason. And to drive home her point even further, Sati went to Daksha's festival dressed as a beggar.

Not surprisingly, the first words out of Daksha's mouth upon seeing his daughter were, "So this is how your darling husband, the great Shiva, dresses *you*, a princess!" By all accounts, Daksha let loose a stream of invective against Shiva in the presence of all his guests. In return, Sati scorned her father and grew so angry that she drew all the heat in her body to one spot and dropped dead.

When Shiva learned of Sati's death, he completely lost his

temper. Shiva, as we know, is called the Destroyer. Shiva called his own court together and led a raid on Daksha's palace, destroying the place, trampling the guests, and smashing Daksha's possessions. Then Shiva lifted the body of his wife over his shoulder and walked around the world.

Shiva was so consumed by grief that all vegetation withered and died wherever he trod. Famine soon overtook the people, and the situation became so grave that the gods feared the destruction not only of all life, but of the entire cosmos. The other gods weren't terribly pleased with Shiva over his behavior at Daksha's palace, but faced with the possible destruction of the universe, they knew that they had to appease him. So they assembled and went to see Brahma the Creator and Vishnu the Preserver. Brahma listened carefully and explained the Great Mystery of the Trimurti.

The Great Mystery of the Trimurti is that the three forces of creation (Brahma), destruction (Shiva), and preservation (Vishnu), were all really one, as they were merely different aspects of the Eternal One, Brahma. In this instance, action was necessary, but Vishnu alone could resolve this situation.

Vishnu reasoned with Shiva. One of Shiva's attendants had cut off Daksha's head, so Vishnu requested that Shiva restore it. Shiva agreed, but he replaced Daksha's human head with that of a goat. Still, Vishnu was determined to save life on the planet. He took his magic discus blade and repeatedly threw it at the body of Sati, cutting it into fifty-two pieces that were scattered around India, each of which became a center of worship of the Great Mother Goddess. This is also why there are fifty-two weeks in a year. Also, some say this is the reason that there are usually fifty-two days between the harvest and the next planting.

With the burden removed from his back, Shiva went beyond

the Himalayas to meditate until the time of the destruction of the world is ordained. Sati was reborn as Uma, the daughter of the Himalayas and the Mother Goddess; in this form, she again married Shiva.

Connections

This is once again a nature myth, a myth of human nature, and a history of prehistory. The story of Daksha's twenty-seven daughters and his son-in-law Soma's (the moon) periodic bouts of consumption are an explanation of the waning and waxing moon along a twenty-seven- or perhaps twenty-eight-day cycle. The body of Sati is cut into fifty-two pieces, each of which becomes a center of worship of the Great Mother Goddess and an explanation of both why there are fifty-two weeks in a year and fifty-two days between the last harvest and next planting in India.

The story bears strong similarity to the Kore myth and the relationship between human life and vegetal life. When Sati dies, the god Shiva (like Demeter) is so grieved that plants and animals die of neglect; after life returns through the actions of Vishnu, Sati is reborn as the Mother Goddess (a patroness of the crops and of childbirth, roughly corresponding to Demeter).

In creating this myth of human nature, the people of ancient India noticed something that we see very often today in a parent-child relationship: the parent and child who do not get along are, in reality, very similar in disposition and emotional structure. Here both Daksha and Sati are equally determined to get their own way.

On a deeper level, there is the statement in response to

human finitude. The young beauty Sati must die before she can be gloriously reborn as the Mother Goddess; indeed, the crops, too, must die before this transformation takes place. The grief of the god, which leads to the death of the crops, is the prelude to Sati's rebirth. As such, we find a familiar statement of the processes surrounding human mortality. Upon the death of a loved one we are consumed by grief, neglecting all other tasks and responsibilities, as we are shocked by the finitude of human life. Yet, beyond that grief, there is transcendence and new life. We are "reborn" through the transcendence we experience in the loss of a loved one.

Another interpretation of this myth comes from the Sanskrit (and subsequently, Hindi) language. *Daksha* is related to the Sanskrit word for *south*, or *dakshin* in modern Hindi. This myth is a possible "history of prehistory," when the invading Aryans entered India from the north and encountered resistance from the native Dravidians of the south. No doubt, the "Dakshas" of the south were reluctant to give tribute to the rulers and gods of the invaders; no doubt, in time, the royal houses intermarried as well.

KLOSKURBEH (OR GLOOSKAP) CAPTURES THE SUMMER
(Algonquin)

The Algonquin peoples of North America were a linguistic family that covered a vast area from the Atlantic to the prairies. They shared a mythology that featured the Great Teacher of the People, variously called Nanabush, Glooskap, or Kloskurbeh. This version of the Algonquin story comes to us from the Abenaki of

Maine, a place where the contrasts between summer and winter are clear.

Once, Kloskurbeh (or Glooskap), the Great Teacher of the People, wandered far to the north and rested at the lodge of an old giant named Winter. Winter observed the usual rituals of hospitality; he fed his guest a sumptuous meal and attempted to entertain Kloskurbeh with long, somewhat boring stories. But, as anyone can tell you, Winter makes people and animals sleepy, so Kloskurbeh fell into a deep, deep sleep that lasted six months.

When he awoke, Kloskurbeh couldn't wait to leave the lodge of Winter, so he took long strides to get south as quickly as possible. He kept on his journey until he smelled flowers and heard insects buzzing and knew that he had arrived at the realm ruled by Summer, a tiny fairy maiden who somewhat resembled a hummingbird. Although tiny, she was the most beautiful thing he had ever seen, and he decided to abduct her.

Kloskurbeh used stealth to creep up on Summer and then tie her up with deerskin thongs, leaving one end of the thongs dragging on the ground as he fled. Summer's tiny subjects, ants and other insects, grasped one end of the thong and tried to free her. Mosquitoes buzzed in Kloskurbeh's face. But the harder the insects pulled and the more the flying insects buzzed, the tighter Kloskurbeh held Summer to his chest. Eventually he slipped her into his pocket and strode northward.

With Summer secreted in his pocket, Kloskurbeh returned to the lodge of Winter, who was once again hospitable and began telling his usual tiresome yarns. This time, however, Winter was surprised to see that Kloskurbeh did not become sleepy. Indeed, the magic of Summer was so great that the lodge of Winter began to melt. Soon, where Winter's icy lodge had once stood, green plants and flowers popped up through the melting snow. Winter himself fled to the north.

After the flowers appeared, Kloskurbeh set Summer free. However, despite the abduction, Summer had become fond of Kloskurbeh, and so visits him every year for three months. She rides in on the wings of the wild geese and leaves with them in autumn. Once she leaves, Winter feels safe to return to his lodge.

Connections

Many of the stories of the origin of the seasons contain the abduction of a female by a male, as does this myth. Summer, like women, bears life. And in the Kore myth, the story of Sati, and this myth, the woman is also the bearer of cyclical rebirth. We see summer travel north on the wings of the geese in spring and return south in the autumn. Of course, this is an obvious nature myth, as anyone in the eastern half of the United States knows from hearing the honking Canada geese in their migratory path. The aquatic bird is a partner in creation in the Algonquin myths, and summertime stimulates a re-creation of the world.

But there is an element of human nature to be considered as well. The bird is often a messenger, as it is at home in the worlds of sky, land, and sea. Even as the aquatic bird appears as a partner in creation in Algonquin myth, it also appears as a guide, messenger, and protector. It is a symbolic bird, indicating that "something" in our depths can cause us to be reborn.

IDUN AND SKADI
(Norse)

The Germanic or Teutonic peoples would certainly place importance on the myths of spring, as their cold homelands included Germany, the Low Countries, and Scandinavia. It is in the Norse outpost of Iceland—the last of the Teutonic countries to be converted to Christianity—that Teutonic mythology persisted longest and in its purest form.

The tales of Idun and Skadi come to us from the Icelandic sagas, again from a people familiar with harsh winters who long for summer.

Idun, the goddess of spring, was the wife of Braggi, god of poetry. It is said of Idun that she had neither a birth nor a death. She carried a basket of apples that temporarily conferred the gift of immortality, warding off age, disease, and fatigue. She would distribute her apples among the gods; afterward, the same number of apples she had started with always remained in the basket.

Once the gods Loki, Honir, and the mighty Odin made one of their periodic trips to earth. They wandered for quite some time and became hungry. Spying a herd of cattle grazing nearby, they slaughtered an ox for a feast. They built a roaring fire and began to roast the ox on the spit. However, despite the roaring flames, the meat did not cook. They hurled more and more wood on the fire, but still the beef remained raw.

The gods were puzzled. They looked up at the sky, saw a huge eagle perched in a nearby tree, and asked it for an explanation. The eagle admitted that it had kept the meat from cooking in order to obtain a portion of the ox for itself. The eagle then offered to help the gods cook the meat; it flapped its wings, making the fire roar and cooking the meat to perfection. Then the eagle went to claim the biggest portion for itself. This angered Loki, who then fought the bird to retrieve the best meat.

Loki grabbed a stake to beat the eagle, but as it was a magical bird, the stake fixed to the eagle's back. The eagle then flew into the air with Loki clinging on. The eagle retaliated by flying low over thistles to torment Loki and banging Loki against the rocks. Loki's body ached and his arms grew tired from holding on. Finally, he simultaneously begged for mercy and tried to cut a deal.

The eagle was actually Thjassi, the storm giant and perennial enemy of the gods. Thjassi agreed to free Loki for a price: Loki was to swear an oath to provide him with Idun's apples of immortality. Loki quickly agreed in order to save his own hide, as he was known to do.

When Loki returned to Asgard, abode of the gods, he dared not tell of his oath. True to his ever duplicitous nature, Loki began to scheme about how he would obtain Idun's apples for Thjassi. When Idun's husband Braggi was away, Loki approached Idun with a beautiful crystal bowl full of ordinary apples. He told her that he had found a magic tree of apples just like Idun's and offered to show the tree to her. Now, as spring is the season of youth and youth is always innocent, Idun gullibly followed Loki out of Asgard. Just then, Thjassi, again in the form of an eagle, carried Idun off to his home in Thrymheim, a cold and desolate place. There Idun was miserable, weeping and refusing to let Thjassi even taste her magic apples.

At first the gods of Asgard merely assumed that Idun had accompanied Braggi on a journey and never gave her absence a second thought. As her absence lasted longer and longer, however, the gods began to feel the ravages of aging: first a few aches and pains, then fatigue, then graying hair. Thor, so proud of his red locks, was going bald . . . and what was left was turning gray! When Braggi returned without Idun, concern turned into panic. They also noticed that Loki remained curiously silent about Idun's absence. For Loki to be quiet at all was a rare enough occasion that it was assumed that he had something to hide yet again.

When the gods asked Loki for an explanation, he tried to change the subject, then feigned ignorance, and then vowed to use all of his wile and cunning in order to find and return Idun to Asgard (without ever fully admitting his own responsibility). Loki borrowed Freya's falcon-feather coat and flew off to rescue Idun. Thjassi was out fishing when Loki arrived. As Loki cleared the walls around Thjassi's home, he turned Idun into a hazelnut. Why a hazelnut? A nut looks dead during the winter, but when planted in spring, it comes back to life and grows into a sapling. Loki then clutched the hazelnut and hastened to Asgard.

Thjassi returned home to find that Idun was gone. He assumed the guise of an eagle and spied Loki off in the distance. In Asgard, the gods could see that Loki was returning and that Thjassi was in hot pursuit. The gods collected wood to build fires on the walls of Asgard. Once Loki and Idun were safely within the walls, the fires were ignited, and the smoke and flames caused Thjassi to become confused, falling to the ground where the gods killed him.

Some time later, Skadi, Thjassi's daughter and the goddess of winter, appeared in Asgard asking for satisfaction for the death of her father. Skadi had a beautiful, but strange appearance; she glistened like stars and had white hair like an old woman but was obviously young. Her touch alone was so cold that it could kill a mortal. She demanded nothing less than another life in exchange for that of her father. Odin pointed to the stars and showed how the gods had honored Thjassi; one could still see his eyes blazing in the heavens. This did not satisfy her. Then Odin suggested that Skadi choose a husband from the ranks of the gods. Skadi was blindfolded, but was still able to see the feet of the assembled deities. She saw one particularly beautiful pair of feet, which belonged to Njörd, the god of the sea breezes. She fell in love with him, and the two were promptly married. By marrying Njörd, she had exacted the price of a life for a life.

When Njörd took Skadi to his home, however, she became very unhappy. The constant sounds of gulls, pounding waves, and surf rushing against the rocks began to get on her nerves. But Njörd had come to love Skadi very much, and so agreed to spend half the year with her in her cold homeland and the other half in his warm kingdom of the gentle sea breezes.

There is another story of Idun. Idun once climbed Yggdrasil, the World Tree, to get a better glimpse of the cosmos. She perched herself far out on a branch for a better view, became dizzy looking down, and plunged all the way down to Niflheim, abode of the dead, ruled by cruel Hel (cognate of English *hell* and German *Hölle*). It wasn't long before the gods missed Idun and went to see her. She was overcome by the coldness of Niflheim and the horrendous sights to be seen there. She shivered and tears ran down her cheeks. Her husband Braggi brought a white wolfskin to cover her and keep her warm. Braggi asked the other gods to return to Asgard without him; he would stay with Idun until she was recovered

and ready to leave. While Braggi and Idun remained in Niflheim, a frost settled over the earth and the birds stopped
singing.

Although Idun eventually returned to Asgard, the memory
was so strong that each year, when the leaves fall and many
birds fly south, a frost settles over the land to remind us of
Idun's fall.

Connections

In the nature myths of Idun, we again see a connection
between spring and immortality. There is also the struggle
between innocence and cunning, spring and cold, and life and
death. Like Kore and Summer, Idun is violently abducted, for
at the moment of death, it often appears that life has been
wrenched out of the body of the dying. The sudden transformation that takes place as the last breath is taken can certainly
appear to be an abduction of the life force. Idun's apples ward
off the effects of aging and decay, even as Idun's fall from the
World Tree into the depths of death's abode heralds the "little
death" of winter's frost. Before the life-force powers of growth
and immortality can be restored, the innocent one must pass
into the realm of death in the underworld.

Idun, the naive, perpetually young bearer of the apples of
immortality, falls into the realm of the mortal dead and lies
there, suspended in shock. But we find Idun, even as we find
ourselves, knowing *about* death, but not *knowing* death. Idun
is immobile and paralyzed; this knowledge is too much for her
to bear. So, too, people, and particularly the young and innocent, find death more difficult to bear. Others try to help us,
but we are stunned; the truth of human finitude is too much to
bear. We survive these grief-filled situations, even transcend

them, but we are never the same as before. In our process of becoming, we have crossed a border into a new frame of existence, a new step in our process of becoming. The pain of finitude and loss is a catalyst for the process of becoming.

From this standpoint, one may discuss the symbolism of the white wolfskin that appeared in the latter myth. In many ancient cultures, it was natural to cover a person (especially a child) who had suffered from exposure with an animal skin, often a fleece, not merely to warm them, but to comfort and revive them. This practice is commonly found in ancient Greece as well. The white wolfskin symbolizes both the white of purity and the carnivorous nature of the wolf. Our grief in falling suddenly into a death leaves us helpless; it is consuming, as is the wolf, but it purifies us. Through it, we learn who we are. The wolf, as in Fenris, the wolf of Norse myth, is a tragic figure, the portent of the Twilight of the Gods, or the time when Fenris becomes harbinger of their doom. Idun, as we are, was purified by tragedy and covered by those who loved her. Thus the myth is brutally frank: we are purified by the tragic, covered by loved ones, but it is reality alone that can revive us. The only way out is through. The innocence of Idun is not lost but transformed into new knowledge; the comfort that revives her is the purity of grasping reality, bitter though it may be. As Jaspers wrote, tragedy is not enough. Its transcendent power and the power of love to transform needs a grasp of the reality of our finitude—that death is the non-negotiable price of life—to work. Idun again becomes the bearer of immortality, but immortality only means something when it opposes death. Idun will not stray again; she knows the power of spring, of life opposed to death. Meaning arises out of the tragic only when faced with the tragic; transcendence cannot be found without the tragic.

AMATERASU HIDES IN HER CAVE
(Japan)

This myth comes to us from the *Kojiki, Records of Ancient Matters,* a history of Japan that includes the genealogical tables from the gods of creation down to the emperors. The myth is used as the basis for an important ritual in modern Japanese Shinto. One often sees tiny bits of white paper or cloth (symbolic of the curved jewels) tied to branches of the *sasaki* pine in memory of Amaterasu's emergence from the cave. The paper and cloth "jewels" are prayers to Amaterasu for prosperity and well-being.

In the beginning were the August Ancestor Gods, the First Two, who created the islands of Japan by stirring the sea. They were Izanagi (Inviting Male) and Izanami (Invited Female). (Note: The last part of Izanami's name refers to the action of the sea waves [as in *tsunami*], and the last part of Izanagi's name refers to the quiet sea. Thus, this is a statement of the Japanese concept of yin and yang, with the male as the active [even destructive] force and the female as the peaceful [and creative] force, a major theme in this story.) After the First Two invented sex by his noticing that he had a little extra flesh between his legs, while she appeared to have a little less, they produced many gods and goddesses before the death of Izanami.

After Izanagi went to the underworld of the dead (Yomi) to see his wife, he needed to ritually purify himself by bathing in a sacred pool. As he washed his right eye, Amaterasu, the sun goddess, was born. As he washed his left eye, Tsukiyomi, the moon goddess, was born. When he washed his nose, Susanowo, the god of storms and winds, was produced.

Amaterasu, or more correctly, Amaterasu-no-kami, ancestress of the emperors of Japan, was the founder of culture; the enemy of culture was the wind god Susanowo, and their sibling rivalry almost destroyed the cosmos. In the time before the gods descended from their heavenly world, Susanowo was a vile, destructive trickster. Amaterasu once gave a lavish banquet for the gods, which Susanowo disrupted by throwing manure and blowing filth everywhere. Susanowo then threw a flayed horse into Amaterasu's fine soiree. Even worse, he destroyed the heavenly rice fields by blowing and causing the irrigation ditches to fill up with silt; opening the floodgates; and scattering the precious rice seed everywhere.

Susanowo's pranks both depressed and angered Amaterasu, who then hid in a cave, depriving the world of light. Everywhere was darkness; as living things need the sun to live, they began to die. The gods were filled with despair over the fate of the cosmos and assembled in front of the cave entrance to coax Amaterasu out of hiding.

First, they sent a host of nocturnal birds to sing at the mouth of the cave; Amaterasu wouldn't come out. Then the gods planted her favorite evergreen tree, the *sasaki*, in front; still she wouldn't leave. They hung beautiful curved jewels and a mirror on the tree, as the sun is always attracted by a mirror; Amaterasu remained hidden.

To relieve the tension, the goddess Ama-no-Uzume did a silly, sexy striptease dance that caused all of the gods to roar with laughter. It was this laughter that finally brought Amaterasu out of the cave, for laughter always chases away the darkness. The other gods then strung a rope across the mouth of the cave to keep Amaterasu from reentering it.

After this, the gods imposed a *harai* (the ritual requirement of compensation) on Susanowo. They plucked out his hair, eyebrows, toenails, and fingernails before commanding him to offer Amaterasu one thousand tables of offerings, including his assistance in working with the sun goddess to ensure the proper growth and ripening of the crops. For the most part, Susanowo has remained reasonably well behaved since this time, but has been known to be his old destructive self occasionally.

Connections

The contest between Amaterasu and Susanowo is the story of the struggle between the creative and destructive. As in the tale of Kore, the gods become upset and all life is put in jeopardy. And this myth also functions as a myth of nature, a myth of human nature, and a "history of prehistory."

As a nature myth, the story of Amaterasu in her cave is most often interpreted as a description of a solar eclipse. Traditionally the Japanese responded to a solar eclipse by singing songs of praise—the *norito* directed to Amaterasu. The story may also be the distant memory of an even greater darkness caused by volcanic activity, wherein the quantity of ash was so great that the sun seemed to disappear. Given the volcanic geography of Japan and the occurrence of this phenomenon even in our own time, this possible interpretation combines the nature myth with a history of prehistory.

We can see other interesting similarities to the nature myth of Kore. Amaterasu's hiding in the cave was similar to Kore's residing in the underworld, and in both myths there was the resulting death of vegetation; a connection between a goddess and agriculture; and the pleadings of the gods to save life on the earth.

This is also clearly a myth about both universal human nature and the nature of human relations in Japan. It is a clear statement of the tension between the destructive and the creative elements present in each of us, the ability of laughter to end darkness, and even the human search for justice. There is a symbolic death and resurrection as Amaterasu climbs down from the heavens to hide in the cave, causing all life to be in peril, only for life to flourish upon her return.

The Japanese, however, read this story differently. This is a story of the tension between personal feelings and one's *on* (Japanese for *duties, loyalties,* and *obligations*). In the Japanese reading of this myth, the gods are perceived as acting to bring Amaterasu out of her personal anger in order to once again resume her *on* as sun goddess, thus completing her role and obligations in both the cosmos and the community of gods. Traditionally, the Japanese consider the fulfillment of *on* the essential statement of personal and social ethics; one's identity is literally that of one's *on*. Interestingly, not only humans and the gods have *on*, but trees, birds, and even the tiny bacteria that cause decay live out their prescribed *on*. The story seeks to establish this as a cosmic and not merely human principle. The *on* of the goddess Amaterasu is to have the sun shine for all of nature. The traditional Japanese ethic is that the order of the cosmos depends on the fulfillment of *on*.

This myth is also the prologue to the Japanese founding myth, wherein Amaterasu is the ancestress of the emperors and establishes the imperial *on*. The mirror and curved jewel that were used to lure Amaterasu from the cave are two of the three emblems of the emperor's legitimacy. (Note: The third is a sword that Amaterasu is said to have given to her descendant Ninigi, as founder of the Japanese state.) Thus, this myth speaks to one's personal and collective identity in the cosmos that is crucial to a sense of meaning in human life.

Many Japanese scholars have interpreted this story as a history of prehistory in a number of ways. The most common of these interpretations is that Amaterasu represents the Yamato kingdom of ancient Japan, who were indeed sun worshipers and were a peaceful, agricultural people. The Japanese national identity is based on a view of the Japanese people as the Yamato race. At one point in time the Yamato were threatened by the warlike people of the kingdom of Izumo, represented by Susanowo. Thus, the myth is symbolic of the victory of culture (as typified by the Yamato) over war (the Izumo).

Another similarity to the Kore myth is that some scholars believe the story to be the record of a struggle between a matriarchy and a patriarchy, wherein the matriarchy is victorious. Indeed, early Japanese history lists many strong queens and empresses, even more than one sees evident in ancient Western culture.

TE ATARAHI
(New Zealand)

The Maori of New Zealand are part of the vast Malayo-Polynesian language and cultural sphere that stretches from Madagascar, through Indonesia and the Philippines, to Tahiti and Hawaii, and thence to the Easter Islands off the coast of Chile. Astonishingly, these vast distances were negotiated millennia ago in small outrigger canoes.

The Polynesian myths are believed to be part of the great southern diffusion of myths from Africa eastward through Polynesia, perhaps even to the Americas, and touching on southern

India. Not surprisingly, the linkage between vegetation and human life is a key theme.

This story from the Polynesian Maori of New Zealand is a simple tale of resurrection with a complex meaning.

There was once a man named Te Atarahi who remained in the underworld for five days and nights and then returned to life. On the fifth day after his death, some women were out cutting leaves in order to make cloth and noticed that someone or something had been sucking the juice out of the flowers. Then they caught sight of a man who strongly resembled the late Te Atarahi, but the hair was gone from the back of his head, and his skin hung loosely on his bones.

Afraid and excited, the women ran back to the village to tell everyone what they had seen. The men refused to believe it and scoffed at the story. But the women were so persistent that the men decided to investigate. The first thing they did, of course, was to see that Te Atarahi's grave remained undisturbed. It was, but there was also a curious small hole near the grave.

Suddenly, to their astonishment, the men saw Te Atarahi seated on a ti log. The ti log is interesting in that it can appear completely dead for quite some time until just the right combination of moisture and light causes green shoots to sprout from it.

The sight was so disconcerting that they sought the help of a *tohunga* (the related Hawaiian term is *kahuna*), a holy man conversant in all manner of otherworldly things. The *tohunga* went out to Te Atarahi and chanted for several days. The people of the village then brought Te Atarahi some food to

eat. The combination of food and chanting caused Te Atarahi
to regain the form of a human being.

Thereafter, Te Atarahi again took his place in village life
and became a popular storyteller and even something of a
tourist attraction. His stories told of how he had met his
departed loved ones in the underworld, but they had informed
him that it was not yet his time to die. Therefore, they
exhorted him not to eat the food of the underworld lest he be
required to remain among the dead forever.

Connections

This story has many parallels, some obvious and some less so.
First, there is the obvious association between the revival of
vegetation (as in the case of the ti log) and the resurrection of
the human body. Secondly, as in the Kore myth, Te Atarahi
was warned not to eat the food in the land of the dead. But,
differently, eating food in the land of the *living* is part of the
process of reviving him. Te Atarahi was welcomed back into
the village not only because of his own resurrection, but as the
hope of life after death that speaks to human finitude.

This myth has interesting parallels with the gospel account
of the resurrection of Jesus. It was women who first saw and
reported on the resurrection of Jesus, only to face skepticism
on the part of the men. Here the women report the news of Te
Atarahi. As in the Kore, Kloskurbeh, Sati, Amaterasu, and
Idun stories, women are the bearers of life as mothers and the
bearers of the news of the return of life.

Now why was there a patch of hair missing at the back of Te
Atarahi's head? The Polynesians believe that the soul could
either pass through the feet or out through the crown of the

head. Obviously, this was the point where Te Atarahi's soul had left the body.

The myths of nature and human nature reflect a worldview different from our own, yet have a poignant familiarity. Unlike ourselves, traditional peoples saw themselves as "in nature" as opposed to distinct from it. While we speak of an environment somehow separate from ourselves, traditional peoples thought in terms of life that included all life and natural forces.

As we have seen, herein was their hope. If there is no distinction between human life and all other life, the periodic renewal of the earth and bursting forth of life in the spring certainly were assurances of human immortality. As surely as the dead seed would appear as next spring's young shoot, human life could not end at death.

As this chapter concerns itself with humanity's collective identity in the cosmos, the next chapter is concerned with the individual struggle for existence, a struggle that is heroic for each of us.

4. Myths of the Hero

The myths of the hero offer an eternal mirror in which we see ourselves. The myths of the hero speak to all the elements of human meaning. The hero is always finite; the hero can *die*. The hero, like ourselves, feels estranged from the numinous, and only in moments of "opening," revelation, and transcendence do we see the gods address or aid the hero; invariably it is in the most tragic moment that this transcendence occurs. The hero is faced with the freedom and burden of choice; the hero makes wrong choices, suffers fatal consequences, and finds himself in ethical dilemmas; it is the very act of choice that makes a hero a hero. The hero is defined in relation to others. The hero speaks to our identity and participation in the cosmos, as the hero myths are always a cultural expression of values and identity.

In considering the hero myths that follow, we should recall heroic elements in some of the myths we have already read. In the tale of Tristan and Isolde, Tristan bears all the signs of a mythic hero. Tristan was born to a royal father who dies and leaves him in the care of a faithful foster father; the hero is always born of a divine, or at least royal, father by a

mortal mother. This is true of the myths we are about to consider: Theseus, Cuchulain, Quetzalcoatl, and Okuninushi. For
example, Cuchulain is the son of Lugh, the sun god, and a
mortal, albeit royal, woman and is raised by a foster father. In
the Judeo-Christian cultural traditions, the stories of Jesus
and Moses both share this pattern. Jesus is both royal and
divine, and raised by a faithful foster father (Saint Joseph).
Moses, destined to lead Israel to freedom and receive the laws
on Mount Sinai, is born to simple parents, but raised in the
Pharaoh's household. This is a universal pattern in the myth
of the hero.

What is the meaning of this divine or royal parentage in
our own lives? It speaks to our finitude and identity. Many of
our cultural traditions address God as "Our Father," and we
see the spark of divinity or the fingerprints of our Creator on
ourselves. Yet still we are mortals with finite sight and short
lives. Our feet are on earth as we gaze at the heavens.

Most of the heroes discussed in this chapter are part divine,
but not actually gods. Yet we include the heroic Norse gods,
Odin and Thor. Why? Unlike the gods of other cultures, the
Scandinavian gods are *heroic gods:* all finite and under a death
sentence; their divine immortality is itself finite. All the Norse
gods know the inevitability of their own destruction in the
Twilight of the Gods. Unlike the gods of other cultures, the
Norse gods pay high prices for their wisdom. The Norse gods,
like ourselves, *become* wise through struggle and suffering, for
of all the aspects of the human condition, none is so poignant
as the costs of our process of becoming.

Each hero included within this chapter is born to greatness,
but always faces trials in order to *become a hero*; he becomes a
hero as life changes him. This inner change is often demonstrated by an outward change of the hero's name. As we have

already seen, Abram's name is changed as he becomes the patriarch Abraham. So, the boy Setanta becomes the hero Cuchulain, and Prince Tonantzin becomes Quetzalcoatl, the Plumed Serpent.

Heroes always demonstrate their prodigy as children and are perceived as a threat. Before the hero has the chance to become a hero, this perceived threat always bears a risk of annihilation by the status quo. In the Jewish tradition, baby Moses is committed to the water in order to save him from Pharaoh's order to kill the male Hebrew children. In the Christian Gospels, Jesus is taken by Joseph and Mary to Egypt after the Three Wise Men inform the jealous King Herod that a king has been born and Herod orders the murder of all Jewish boys under the age of two. Medea attempts to poison Theseus before he can gain his rightful throne. Cuchulain's first battle is against the boy warriors sent by his own uncle, King Conchobar. Okuninushi is set upon by his own father. The myth of the hero is a mirror of our own heroic struggles for individuality, creativity, and self-expression.

The hero makes promises that he cannot keep without destroying either himself or someone he loves. The hero is bound by laws and taboos; he cannot keep one without violating another. Thus, the hero carries the burdens of choice that we carry in our own lives. For Theseus and Cuchulain, the price of choice is death.

The hero is subject to the betrayal of either a friend or a brother, sometimes merely the result of cruel fate, at other times the result of jealousy or lust. In this we think of lost friendships and our own moments of feeling betrayed. Judas becomes a byword for *traitor* in betraying Jesus with a kiss. Ferdia betrays the beloved "brother," Cuchulain, for the love of a woman, and Theseus rashly first accuses his own son of betrayal, only to be betrayed himself, causing Theseus's death. Love always bears the potential of betrayal in each human life, often with great subtlety and ambiguity. Often what appears to be betrayal is that two people's processes of becoming meet a fork in the road and take different paths. Nowhere is this more poignantly illustrated than in the myths of the hero.

The hero makes the journey to the underworld, the land of the dead, and returns. The hero faces what Kierkegaard called "the dark night of the soul" or "the sickness unto death"; he is defeated, shamed, his spirit crushed, and his very sense of feeling as a hero debased. The hero finds himself in a time of dryness, a spiritual desert. Yet in these moments, the numinous appears and transcendence allows the hero to again take up the quest. It is to a battle-weary, aching, bleeding, crushed Cuchulain that his father, Lugh the sun god, appears quite literally as a light in the darkness. Cuchulain's experience of the numinous allows him to fight again. Like the people of Israel, the route to the promised land is through the barren desert.

These are *our* stories.

THESEUS
(Greece)

There is an intriguing historical perspective to this myth. During the 1890s, Sir Arthur Evans excavated the royal palace at Knossos, Crete. There was, in 2000 B.C., an enormous difference in the level of development on Crete relative to that of mainland Greece. Evans found flush toilets and advanced plumbing in the palace—advancements not in common use again in western Europe until the end of the nineteenth century. More important to our study, the labyrinthine hallways of the palace, the many depictions of bullfights, and the evidence of commerce with the Greek mainland all add veracity to the story of Theseus, an early king of Athens.

To a simple visitor from Bronze Age Greece, the vast corridors of the palace must have seemed like a maze; the sight of men riding bulls would have easily given rise to the Minotaur—a half-man, half-bull monster.

The Birth and Youth of Theseus

King Aegeus of Athens had two wives, Melite and Chaciope, neither of whom provided him with an heir. Aegeus traveled to Corinth, where he consulted with the sorceress Medea. She agreed to provide Aegeus with the magic necessary to sire a son in exchange for his promise that he would offer her protection and asylum in Athens, to which he readily agreed.

At the town of Troezen, en route back to Athens, Aegeus had an affair with Aethra, a woman of the blood of the royal house of Athens. He warned her that if this liaison were to produce a son, she must keep the child in Troezen and secretly raise him there so that his wife would never know of the tryst. Aegeus then placed his sandals and sword under a rock sacred to Zeus; his future heir would prove himself by finding this "deposit." The true son of Aegeus would be able to lift the rock and bring these tokens to Athens as a demonstration of his claim to the throne.

Unknown to Aegeus, Aethra gave birth to a boy, naming

him Theseus *(deposited)*. She recalled the tokens of kingship that her lover had deposited under the sacred rock, and waited until the child grew strong and wise, showing that he had the favor of the gods. She told Theseus of the deposit, and with great ease, he lifted the rock and removed the tokens of kingship. He then set out for Athens to make his claim to the throne. But the roads between Troezen and Athens were plagued with bandits; thus, Theseus had his first heroic task to perform.

The first bandit he met was Epidaurus the Lame, known for killing hapless travelers with a brass club and then taking their money. When Epidaurus tried to attack Theseus, he met his match at last: Theseus seized the brass club and slew Epidaurus.

The second bandit was the wretched Sinis Pityocamtes (Sinis the Pine-bender). This man used to bend the tops of pine trees low with his great strength, then ask travelers to give him a hand in his work. When the traveler had a good grip on the top of the pine tree, Sinis would let go. The traveler would then be flung through the air only to either fall to his death or be catapulted into sharp rocks. Theseus used his own great strength to kill Sinis in the same manner that Sinis killed his victims.

The third bandit was Sciron *(parasol)*, who forced his victims to wash his feet, then when they were bent down, he kicked them into a steep gorge into the sea, where they were eaten by turtles. Theseus meted Sciron the same fate.

Theseus was considered by the Athenians to be the father of Greek wrestling after demonstrating his mastery of Cercyon, an evil bandit who challenged every traveler to a wrestling match that always concluded with Cercyon dashing his opponent's head against a rock. Cercyon was dealt the same fate by

Theseus. Then Theseus neared the outskirts of Athens, where he killed a fierce wild boar that had claimed many lives.

News of Theseus's exploits preceded him to Athens, where the people were thrilled to be rid of the bandits and the boar.

However, many years had passed since King Aegeus had been in Troezen where Theseus was conceived. The king did not know that he had such a son. Meanwhile, Medea had been driven from Corinth and fled to Athens, where Aegeus had assured her asylum. Aegeus had taken Medea as his third wife, and they had a son, Medus, whom Aegeus erroneously considered the son and heir whom Medea had foretold.

When news of Theseus's exploits had reached the palace, Aegeus had no idea that this hero was his son, and feared that Theseus would prove a dangerous rival to his rule. Medea, however, knew exactly who Theseus was, and was afraid that the hero would take the throne away from her son. Aegeus and Medea knew that they had no choice but to welcome Theseus to Athens, but together they plotted to kill him. So Medea prepared some poison from the wolfsbane plant and placed it in a cup of wine.

During the feasting, Theseus took his sword from the scabbard and used it to cut some meat; it was the same sword that Aegeus had deposited under the rock many years before. Aegeus recognized the sword and recognized that Theseus was his son and true heir. Aegeus immediately knocked the poisoned wine onto the floor and rejoiced, proclaiming Theseus as his heir. Moreover, as Aethra, Theseus's mother, was of the royal blood of Athens, there was no way that Theseus's claim could be contested. Medea became angry with this and thus was sent into exile for her treachery.

Theseus and the Minotaur

Crete is an island off the coast of Greece that was ruled by King Minos. Minos had sent his only son on a diplomatic mission to Athens. The Cretans were known throughout all the world for their skill fighting bulls, and King Aegeus asked the Cretan prince, Androgeus, for help in killing a particularly fierce bull that plagued the Athenian countryside. In the process, Androgeus was killed and all Athens feared the repercussions.

Minos demanded revenge. He invaded Athens and vowed to destroy the city unless the Athenians offered a tribute. When the Athenians offered gold and silver, Minos refused. The only tribute that could compensate for the loss of the Cretan heir to the throne was for the Athenians to send their seven finest young men and as many young women to Crete every nine years. The young Athenians never returned from Crete; they were murdered there by a horrible monster, the Minotaur.

The story of the Minotaur is yet another example of human stupidity toward the gods. King Minos had been given a beautiful white bull by the sea god, Poseidon, who expected it to be returned to him as a sacrifice. Instead, Minos prized the bull and refused to give it up. Poseidon was angry and caused Pasiphae, Minos's wife, to fall in love with the bull. She later gave birth to the horrible Minotaur, who was half human, half bull, and the fiercest creature alive. Minos did not kill the Minotaur. Rather, the king asked Daedalus, the world's greatest builder, to construct a labyrinth, a maze of corridors, in which the monster could be safely kept, and Minos would give the Minotaur human beings to eat. The young Athenians were placed in the hopeless maze and murdered there by the fierce man-beast.

Theseus arrived in Athens during the ninth year of this human sacrifice. He stepped forward and offered to be one of the seven people sent to Crete. His father despaired of sending the heir to the throne on such a mission, but Theseus, reciting his past exploits, assured Aegeus that if anyone could kill the Minotaur, he would, thus ending the slaughter of Athenian youths. So Theseus boarded the ship and left for Crete.

It was understood by the Athenians that they should watch the sail when the ship returned. If the ship returned with a black sail, then all the young Athenians had perished. However, if the ship returned with a white sail, the young Athenians had been spared and were safely aboard.

Upon arriving in Crete, the Athenians were paraded through the streets. Ariadne, daughter of King Minos, fell instantly in love with Theseus and went to Daedalus for assistance in saving the handsome Athenian. Daedalus gave Ariadne a map of the maze, which she studied carefully. She then gave Theseus a ball of string to unwind behind him. By knowing where he had been, Theseus could retrace his steps and escape the labyrinth. Fortunately for the other thirteen young Athenians, Theseus was the first of their party to encounter the Minotaur, whom the hero easily killed with his bare hands.

Thus, the fourteen young Athenians escaped unharmed. Ariadne had received a promise from Theseus that he would take her to Greece with him, where they would marry. On the way, however, she became violently ill and Theseus dropped her off on the island of Naxos. Another version of the story is that she became tiresome and nagging during the voyage and was simply left there. In either case, the ship returned to Athens with all fourteen Athenians on board.

In their haste to return, however, someone forgot to replace the black sail that had graced the ship on its outward journey with the white one. King Aegeus had watched the seas for a sign of the ship. When he saw the black sail as the ship returned, he thought that his son and heir had perished in Crete. In despair, he threw himself to his death in the sea that has been known ever since as the Aegean. Thus, upon the ship's return to Athens, Theseus found himself king.

The hero was acclaimed as the founder of Athenian democracy. Instead of ruling the people himself, he allowed them to rule themselves. He was a wise and beloved king, the patron of culture and commerce. During his reign, skilled artisans and thinkers from all throughout Greece moved to Athens to work under his patronage. Things in Athens were happy and prosperous, as the Cretans no longer demanded tribute. With affairs in good order in his realm, Theseus set out in search of further adventures.

Theseus and Hippolytus

Theseus was married to Phaedra, Ariadne's sister, but he also had a handsome son named Hippolytus by an earlier marriage. Phaedra fell hopelessly in love with Hippolytus and repeatedly tried to seduce him. This came about because Hippolytus's looks had attracted the affections of the goddess Aphrodite, but Hippolytus was a devotee of the perpetually virgin hunt goddess Artemis and not interested in sex. Hippolytus's devotion to Artemis angered the jealous Aphrodite, who now vowed to destroy the youth. It is said that Aphrodite caused Phaedra to fall in love with Hippolytus out of spite.

As Phaedra grew more forceful in demanding the affections of Hippolytus, the boy rebuffed her; it was not right to sleep with one's stepmother. In despair, Phaedra hanged herself, leaving a suicide note claiming that Hippolytus *had* seduced her, causing her despair and death. When Theseus found the note, he was both grieved and disgusted. He prepared to send Hippolytus into exile. When the youth protested that he had done nothing to his stepmother, Theseus refused to believe him. In his anger, Theseus rashly called on Poseidon, god of the sea, to destroy Hippolytus. As Hippolytus set out on his flight from Athens, a sea creature came out of the water in front of his chariot. This frightened the horses, and Hippolytus was fatally thrown from the vehicle.

The dying youth was brought before his father. The goddess Artemis herself appeared to Theseus to tell him that Hippolytus was innocent of any wrongdoing with regard to Phaedra. Artemis explained that Aphrodite had been behind the plot, and that Phaedra had been bewitched; the jealous goddess had planned to destroy Hippolytus for spurning her as well as all other women in his devotion to chastity. Distraught, Theseus begged the gods for mercy.

The gods weighed the evidence. Theseus had done much good for the people of Athens. So the gods were compassionate—up to a point, for no collection of good deeds can atone for causing the wrongful death of another, especially one's own son. The gods decided to postpone Theseus's punishment. (But Theseus, as justice would have it, later died by the treachery of a friend, because he himself was guilty of treachery in believing the lies of Phaedra and cursing his own innocent son.)

Theseus in the Underworld

The sad death of Hippolytus took its toll on the now aging Theseus. He took less interest in the affairs of Athens, and his friend Perithous urged Theseus to join him on a daring new adventure. Perithous persuaded Theseus to join him in traveling to Sparta, where they would abduct Helen, the sister of the Dioscuri, Castor and Polydeuces. (Note: This is not the same Helen as Helen of Troy.) Perithous and Theseus made an oath to protect each other, and once Helen was abducted, the two would draw lots for her.

The Dioscuri were the children of Zeus by a mortal woman, and Theseus thought that if he won Helen, the additional marriage would make a powerful alliance and Theseus would have Zeus himself as a father-in-law. Kings, at that time, married as many wives as politics and desire dictated. Yet both Perithous and Theseus were aware that the Dioscuri brothers would never give Helen up without a fight.

Theseus and Perithous led a small Athenian army to Sparta, where they seized Helen while she was sacrificing to the gods. Theseus and Perithous, true to their oath, cast lots, and Theseus was the winner. However, on closer inspection, Helen was not yet a woman, but still a young girl who had years to go before she would attain a marriageable age. This was disappointing, especially since had Theseus married Helen and produced a child, the Dioscuri might have forgiven him. But now, the Spartan armies were closing in on them!

The two Athenians narrowly escaped, and Theseus left Helen with his mother, Aethra, until she reached puberty. Theseus was now in a great predicament: He had incurred the wrath of the Dioscuri—possibly even of Zeus himself; it would be years before a marriage could forge a strategic alliance with Sparta; and he had begun a blood feud with one of the most powerful families in all Greece. Theseus expected the Spartan armies to attack Athens at any time, but years passed without an attack. Theseus grew more and more paranoid as time passed; he knew that he would have to pay dearly for the abduction of Helen. Moreover, Theseus questioned the wisdom of his vow to Perithous, who grew more and more annoying by asking Theseus to find him a wife.

Theseus's paranoia was not groundless. The Dioscuri, as sons of Zeus, were far too subtle to send an army against Athens. They delighted in hearing reports of the tormented Theseus, groomed their own heir to the Athenian throne, and were confident that their father would design a fitting punishment for Theseus and Perithous. When Helen eventually did come of age and Theseus married her, this only whetted their appetite for revenge.

One day, Theseus and Perithous consulted the oracle of Zeus in order to find Perithous a wife. The oracle sarcastically replied, "Why doesn't Perithous just go to the underworld and marry Persephone? After all, Hades is her husband only part of the year!" The stupid Perithous took this at face value, totally oblivious to the sarcasm, and decided to go to the underworld. When Theseus tried to dissuade Perithous, the latter reminded Theseus of their oath; if Perithous went to the underworld to abduct Persephone, then Theseus was bound to go with him.

Zeus, meanwhile, had never forgiven Theseus for the death of Hippolytus; the abduction of Helen only compounded things. As Zeus and Hades were brothers, they spoke often. One day Zeus informed Hades that the two Athenians were on their way to abduct Persephone. With a cruel smirk, Hades replied, "I'll be ready!"

When Theseus and Perithous arrived in the underworld, they knocked at the door. Cruel and clever as always, Hades bade them welcome, gave a grand speech on what an honor it was to have such distinguished guests, and feigned lavish hospitality. When Hades asked the two Athenians to sit down on a bench, they found their bodies became glued to it, and were completely unable to move. Suddenly, as if from nowhere, hissing serpents slithered toward the bench, Hades' cruel three-headed dog, Cerberus, began ripping at their flesh, and bands of Furies appeared with whips. These agonies endured for four years, providing Hades with grim entertainment.

Word of the horrible torments reached Heracles, who remembered that Theseus alone had defended him when Heracles had temporarily lost his mind and murdered his wife and children. Heracles, himself a son of Zeus, both remained grateful to Theseus and felt that the two Athenians had been punished enough. Moreover, Perithous—and not Theseus— had been the chief culprit in the farcical abduction of Helen.

Persephone, as we know, was never terribly thrilled by spending time with Hades in the underworld, and the cruel punishment of the two Athenians was more than she could bear. When Heracles arrived in the underworld, he told Persephone that he had come to rescue Theseus out of loyalty, but needed help to accomplish his goal. Persephone vowed to leave the gates out of the underworld unlocked for just a few hours, to assist Heracles. But she swore Heracles to absolute secrecy, lest the other souls find out, escape, and create havoc in the world of the living.

Persephone used her charms to lure Hades away from the spectacle of the two miserable Athenians. When Hades left the hall, Heracles approached the bench where Theseus and Perithous pathetically beckoned for help as the tortures continued. Heracles ripped Cerberus from Theseus's body and chased away the serpents with his staff; the Furies had been commanded by Zeus never to afflict Heracles. Heracles took

Theseus in one arm and Perithous in the other, and they hastened to flee the underworld. Theseus climbed on Heracles' shoulder and safely landed in the upper world. Perithous lagged behind, and just as Heracles reached to pull him to safety, the earth swallowed him up and Perithous remained in the underworld forever.

All this was the will of Zeus. Zeus loved Theseus for the many good things Theseus had done for Athens. He remembered Theseus's defense of Heracles with appreciation. Now, while Zeus was displeased by the abduction of Helen, the king of the gods weighed Theseus's deeds on his scales. Zeus felt that the four years in the underworld had paid Theseus's debt for the abduction. Perithous, on the other hand, had only caused misery to others and so deserved to spend more time in the underworld. It had to be so, as Justice is one of the spindles on which the cosmos forever turns. If that spindle breaks, even the gods of Olympus will fall. One score remained unsettled, however: Theseus's responsibility for the death of Hippolytus.

The Death of Theseus

While Zeus had seen fit to allow Heracles to free Theseus, the Dioscuri had not yet forgiven the Athenian for the abduction of Helen. Upon hearing that Theseus was again walking the streets of Athens, they planned to attack the city. The Dioscuri were confident of their ability to launch a successful attack because Athens had deteriorated badly in Theseus's absence. The defenses were weak, a lack of leadership threatened the Athenian democracy, and crime took the place of arts and commerce. Without Theseus there to protect them, the poor were exploited and oppressed.

Even as Athens was not the city that Theseus had left, Theseus was no longer the king he had been. Once Theseus had erected temples to Heracles in gratitude for the rescue, he retired to his court and neglected his duties. He recounted his past glories to anyone willing to listen, wallowed in self-hatred and self-pity over the death of Hippolytus, and drank wine until he was in a stupor.

During Theseus's absence, one Peteos had been groomed by the Dioscuri to rule Athens. Peteos assumed the title of regent during Theseus's four years in the underworld. The Dioscuri were prepared to make Peteos king upon their conquest of Athens. However, Peteos dissuaded the Spartans from attacking, stating that with a little patience, the Athenians themselves would depose Theseus. There would be no resistance by the Athenians to the Dioscuri, Peteos would be king, and not a drop of Spartan blood would need to be shed.

Peteos was right. Theseus neglected the repair of the temples and missed meetings of the Athenian leaders, all the while indulging himself without a single thought to the people of Athens.

Theseus had inherited a valuable estate near the sea, in an area ruled by Lycomedes, who considered Theseus's estate to be rightfully his. Lycomedes invited Theseus to visit the estate, gave the Athenian plenty to drink, and then offered to show Theseus the sights. When the two stopped at a scenic view of the sea from some dramatic cliffs, Lycomedes pushed the drunken Theseus over the side into the sea. Of course, Lycomedes told people that the tipsy Theseus had slipped and fallen to his death . . . in the Aegean Sea where Theseus's own father jumped to his death.

Connections

As in all the classic myths of the hero, Theseus is born of a royal father (and, in this case, mother), but the father absents himself during the hero's childhood. Theseus's quest is to realize his birthright as heir to the Athenian throne. He demonstrates the claim by removing the hidden tokens of kingship from beneath the sacred rock and vanquishing Athens's enemies. As a young hero, Theseus is also perceived by Aegeus as a rival and threatened with annihilation upon his arrival in Athens.

The myth of the Minotaur is an example of the power of the myth of the hero as an allegory of each human life. Theseus must pass many tests before he faces his most significant challenge: defeating the man-bull Minotaur in the middle of the labyrinth, a vast maze. However, with the help of his lover, he is able to know where he has been and can escape from the maze.

For us, myths are a way to know where we have been and work through the complex maze of our own existence. And for us, as for Theseus, love guides us through that maze.

This episode with the maze speaks potently to the elements of human existence that we find in the myth of the hero; it is a mirror of our own lives. Theseus is finite and mortal; death lurks around every corner in the labyrinth. Theseus speaks to our process of becoming; all of his past exploits mean little as he negotiates the maze. And the man who victoriously emerges from the maze is not the same man who entered it.

The tragic tale of Theseus and Hippolytus speaks to the human condition as regards the freedom and burden of choice. Theseus chooses to believe Phaedra's lies about Hippolytus at the very high price of losing his own son and heir. It also speaks to the human condition of estrangement; goddesses are set against each other, and the mortals are their tragic pawns.

This episode is also interesting in that it offers a plot common in the myths of many cultures. The story line is this: an older, married woman attempts to seduce an innocent young man, but is repeatedly rejected. The woman scorned, however, tells her husband that the youth has been attempting to seduce *her*. The husband believes her lies, and the youth faces tragic consequences. This plot, for example, occurs in the Egyptian and Blackfeet Indian Tales of Two Brothers; the Greek myth of Bellerophon; and the Bible story of Joseph and Potiphar's wife.

The myths of the hero often include a journey to the under-world, the land of the dead. On the first look, such myths appear to be a statement of hope that the human spirit can conquer death. While this is true, there is still more.

Throughout the ages, maturity has been defined as a grasp of one's own finitude, of coming face-to-face with one's own mortality. Indeed, the hero usually goes to the underworld relatively late in the myth. The hero faces death, battles it (or in the case of Theseus, escapes it), and returns to the world of the living. But this victory against death is never accomplished by the hero acting *alone*; invariably for the hero, as for us, this victory is accomplished with the loving help of others. Theseus is helpless by himself. Heracles, in loving gratitude for Theseus's past kindness, rescues Theseus. Once again, love is stronger than death.

The very manner whereby Theseus is imprisoned in the underworld speaks to the freedom and burden of human choice. It is only through keeping his vow to Perithous that Theseus is consigned to the tortures and agonies of Hades' kingdom. The episode ends with a hopeful assertion of the eternal principle of divine justice as the spindle whereupon the very wheels of the cosmos turn.

Some mythic heroes die dramatically in battle, but not Theseus. Theseus, the hero, has now stopped being heroic. While the tragic always exists in the heroic narrative, at the end of this myth the heroic is removed, leaving only the tragic. The old Theseus is no longer the hero Theseus. He has neglected the kingdom that was his birthright and earned at great cost. He has forsaken the people, whose champion he once was. His past heroism is a memory; he has refused the heroic call.

The painful irony is that this hero bravely battled without fear of death, even returned from the land of the dead, only to cease being heroic. It is not in battle that Theseus dies, but rather as the result of a treachery recalling Theseus's own treachery against his son. A grim statement is made regarding the human condition: the same divine justice that brought Theseus back from the land of the dead now exacts the price of Theseus's own death when he refuses the heroic call.

CUCHULAIN
(Ireland)

Cuchulain is, unquestionably, the Irish cultural hero, and remains important in Irish literature and national symbolism. Not only was Cuchulain an important theme in the poetry and dramas of W. B. Yeats, but he was invoked as a powerful symbol during the twentieth-century battle for Irish nationalism.

The sources for these myths are the ancient Irish sagas, which constitute the third–oldest source of European literature, surpassed only by the Greeks and Romans.

Cuchulain's Birth and Youth

Cuchulain was the son of the god Lugh and a mortal woman, Deichtne. The birth of Cuchulain was heralded by a great sign: a mare gave birth to twin foals, who later earned glory as Cuchulain's war horses. However, Cuchulain was fathered by the god Lugh in the form of a bird; Deichtne's husband, Sualtam, was thought by most to be his father, and he, knowing the boy's true identity, raised the boy as his own. Cuchulain was raised by three wise men: Sencha, who taught him wisdom; Fergus, who taught him the arts of war; and the druid Cadhbad, who taught him magic.

Cuchulain's hair was black at the roots, red in the middle, and blond at the tips. He had seven pupils in each eye, seven fingers on each hand, and seven toes on each foot. When Cuchulain was not seized by the battle frenzy, however, he was very handsome.

His first signs of heroism came at the age of four, when he journeyed alone to Emhain Mhacha, where 350 boy-warriors raised by Conchobar, his own jealous uncle, attacked him; he easily subdued them. As Cuchulain passed through the land of Culann, he encountered the huge hound that guarded the gates of that country. The giant, fierce hound lashed at the young hero, who happened to be playing with a ball. With his superhuman strength, Cuchulain threw the ball down the hound's throat, then grabbed the vicious creature, dashing it to bits against a stone pillar. Culann

himself emerged from his palace and berated the young hero
for killing his dog. Ever courteous, Cuchulain apologized,
offering to guard the gates himself, which he did for three
days. Previously the young hero had been known as Setanta;
now he received the name Cuchulain—meaning *Culann's
hound.*

All heroes must go through an initiation before going on the
great quest. To learn the lore necessary to undertake his adventures, Cuchulain studied under Cadhbad the Druid, who
taught many incantations and the body of secret wisdom.
Cadhbad also studied the portents and omens and one day declared to Cuchulain that "any hero who takes up arms this
very day, even if he live but a day, the same shall have
his name known forever." Cuchulain immediately went to his
now humbled uncle, King Conchobar, to say that this was the
appointed day for him to take up arms. The hero tried and
destroyed fifteen sets of weapons before Conchobar gave
Cuchulain his own personal arms to take into battle.

Cuchulain then climbed into his war chariot, driven by
Laeg, his faithful chariot driver, and set out on the road south,
out of Ulster. At the border with the province of Connacht,
the three sons of Nechta Scene attacked him. All of Ulster
knew of these fierce warriors; of them it was said that they had
killed as many Ulstermen as remained alive! But Cuchulain
slew them quickly and severed their heads.

To triumphantly return to Ulster, Cuchulain climbed into
his chariot and tied the three heads to its frame. He also cap-
tured a great stag and a flock of swans without killing a single
one. Cuchulain rode toward the court of King Conchobar with
the elk walking behind his chariot and the swans flying over
his head.

In his encounters, first with the boy-warriors and then with

the three sons of Nechta Scene, it was observed that Cuchulain had been seized by a battle frenzy, which made him slay
all comers, whether friend or foe, unless stopped. His countrymen were thus terrified of him and recognized that he had to
be awakened out of his current frenzy before he entered into
King Conchobar's court. First, the Ulster women, led by their
Queen Maeve, ran naked to greet Cuchulain in order to distract him and pull him out of the battle frenzy. This almost
did the trick, but the honorable Cuchulain covered his eyes to
keep from seeing the women's nakedness. Terrified that the
Ulster hero would unwittingly slay his own countrymen and
kinsmen at Conchobar's court, the strongest warriors of Ulster
seized Cuchulain by stealth (when a person is angry or seized
by the urge to violence, stealth always gets them). They threw
him into a great cauldron of water to cool him off, but Cuchulain's battle frenzy was so great that Cuchulain caused the
water to boil! They pulled him from that vat and threw him
into a second, which Cuchulain rendered only tepid. It took a
third vat to bring the hero to his senses, at which time he
apologized for putting his friends and relatives at risk.

When Cuchulain came of age, he went throughout the
land to find a suitable wife. When Cuchulain arrived at Luska
(now New Lusk, near Dublin), Emer, daughter of Forgall,
was busy teaching the ladies of the court the secrets of embroidery. Emer was skilled in all of the six arts of women—
beauty, singing, sweet words, embroidery, wisdom, and
chastity. Whereas many maidens of Ireland wanted to woo
Cuchulain, Emer alone was not interested. At first, Emer told
Cuchulain that the hero should marry her elder sister Fial, as
she, Emer, was the youngest and could not wed first. But it
was not Fial that Cuchulain was interested in, so he continued
to try to coax Emer into marrying him. Finally, Emer told

Cuchulain that she would not marry him until he proved himself a true hero.

So, Cuchulain went to visit Sceatha, a woman warrior who taught young heroes the secrets of battle. To arrive at her home in the land of shadows, one must cross the sea, navigate through dense forests, and cross desolate rocky crags (legend has it that her home is the Isle of Skye in Scotland). As Cuchulain wearily traveled to reach Sceatha, an apparition with a face that shone like the sun came before him; it was his father, Lugh. The apparition gave Cuchulain the gift of a wheel of light and instructed the young hero to follow the wheel where it led him. This took Cuchulain past the most dangerous parts of the journey in complete safety until he came to the Great Leap that was at the frontier of Sceatha's land.

At the approach to the Great Leap, Cuchulain was heartened by the sight of many heroes from his homeland, especially his old friend Ferdia, of the tribe of the Fir Bolg. To cross the gorge of the Great Leap, there was a narrow bridge, but it was enchanted; as one steps on one end of the bridge, the middle snaps back to knock the hapless traveler backward. Many who tried to leap across the gorge fell and were eaten by the sea monsters in the boiling waters below. Three times Cuchulain attempted to cross the bridge and thrice was he thrown back. On the fourth try, he leapt to the middle of the bridge and with another leap arrived at the land of Sceatha. His friend Ferdia was the first to welcome him.

In addition to tactics, swordsmanship, and magic, Sceatha taught the two heroes the secret of the *Gae-bolga*, or belly-weapon, which the warrior flung, using his foot, into the belly of his enemy, causing instant death. Cuchulain forgot all about Emer, however, when Sceatha asked for his help in fighting against the Princess Aife, the greatest woman warrior in the world after Sceatha. Still, Sceatha was reluctant to send Cuchulain into battle, given his lack of experience, so she decided to drug him and allow him to sleep when Aife's troops came. But the potion lasted only an hour, and Cuchulain took up arms; Sceatha was amazed by his skill as a warrior.

Immediately, Cuchulain, with Ferdia's help, slew six of Aife's best warriors. Aife had challenged Sceatha to hand-to-hand combat, but Cuchulain went in place of his tutor. Sceatha told Cuchulain that Aife's weakness was her vanity and the pride she took in her horses and chariot. Aife and Cuchulain fought hard, until with a strategic blow, Aife shattered Cuchulain's sword. All appeared lost, when Cuchulain suddenly cried out, "See how Aife's horses and chariot are running down into the glen!" When Aife turned her head, Cuchulain seized her and held her to the ground, his knife to her throat. Aife begged for her life, so Cuchulain made her promise a lasting, permanent peace with Sceatha. Moved by Cuchulain's bravery, Aife became his lover and bore him a son, Connla. Cuchulain charged his son Connla under the *geissa* (plural of *geis*), a series of ritual taboos; he was never to refuse combat, and never to walk away from any battle against anyone. The violation of the *geissa* meant certain death.

Cuchulain eventually returned to his home at Emhain Macha and married Emer. He had told Emer of his tryst with Aife and the birth of Connla, and Emer knew that the story could have but only one tragic end. Connla was as brave as his father and, bound by the *geissa*, he fought first against King Conor of Ulster, who called for Cuchulain; the boy was too great a match for any of Conor's men. So many years had passed that Cuchulain did not recognize his own son. The lad fought bravely and then Cuchulain used the *Gae-bolga* he had learned from Sceatha and killed Connla. As Connla lay

dying, the boy revealed who he was. Under *geissa*, Connla had
had no choice but to fight against Cuchulain; and it led to his
own death.

> He spake to the young man, "Is there no maid
> Who loves you, no white arms to wrap you round,
> Or do you long for the dim sleepy ground,
> That you have come and dared me to my face?"
> "The dooms of men are in God's hidden place."
> "Your head a while seemed like a woman's head
> That I loved once."
>
>   Again the fighting sped,
> But now the war rage in Cuchulain woke,
> And through that new blade's guard the old blade broke,
> And pierced him.
>
>   "Speak before your breath is done."
>
> "Cuchulain I, mighty Cuchulain's son."
>
> —W. B. Yeats, *Cuchulain's Fight with the Sea*

The Trials of Cuchulain

Bricriu of the Poisoned Tongue, one of the masters of Ulster,
lived to stir up strife among the heroes of Ireland. He decided
to hold a great feast to provide an opportunity to cause discord
by leading his guests to contend between themselves to deter-
mine who was the true champion of Ireland. The three top
contenders were Cuchulain, Conall, and Laery. Bricriu summoned a demon from the depths of a lake to judge between
them. The demon told the three heroes that any one of them
could cut off his head today—provided that the hero would
place his own head on the block tomorrow. Of the three, only

Cuchulain was brave enough to face this test. Immediately, Cuchulain beheaded the demon.

The demon returned the next day and demanded that Cuchulain place his head on the block. When the hero did so, the demon tried three times to cut off the hero's head with his war ax; three times he failed, and Cuchulain rose unhurt. Bricriu's guests all hailed Cuchulain then as the greatest of the heroes.

As Cuchulain was hero of Ulster, the forces of the rival provinces of Connacht and Leinster sought to conquer and subdue the Ulstermen. Connacht was ruled by King Ailill and Queen Maeve, who hated Cuchulain. A vast army was arrayed to attack Ulster. Sadly, Maeve had promised the hand of her daughter, the fair Findabair, to Ferdia on the condition that Ferdia, the beloved friend of Cuchulain, join her against the Ulstermen; tragedy was now inevitable.

Maeve was in possession of a great red bull, Finnbhenach. But Finnbhenach would not remain the possession of a woman, and he went to be with the cows owned by King Ailill of Ulster. Fergus MacRoy, an Ulster traitor, told Maeve of the mighty Brown Bull of Cuilaigne in Ulster, and Maeve had to get possession of the bull, both out of greed and as a means to humiliate the Ulstermen. So she and Fergus connived to lead her amassed forces to invade Ulster to steal the Brown Bull and recover Finnbhenach.

Now one Macha had placed a curse upon all of Ulster, and its heroes lay in agony and pain, unable to lift a spear. When Maeve's druids informed her of this, she called for an immediate invasion.

But Cuchulain's sentries had informed him of the coming armies, and the hero and his foster father, Sualtam, waited on the frontiers of Ulster. But Cuchulain was weak when it came to women, and instead of tending to the defenses, he went to meet a woman for a tryst in the forests. While there, Cuchulain cut an oak sapling using but one hand, closed one eye, stood on one foot, and tied a knotted wreath from it. He then wrote on the wreath in ogham characters that none of the armies of Maeve could enter Ulster unless they had duplicated Cuchulain's wreath. By the rules of *geissa* the armies of Maeve had to respond to the challenge.

As the Connachtmen arrived, they all tried to duplicate Cuchulain's feat, but not a one could do so. Suddenly, a blizzard struck and covered the land with snow. The Connachtmen remained there encamped until the next day. They then interpreted the *geis* as lasting but a day, and continued onward into Ulster.

The snow had been a blessing from the gods: returning from his tryst, Cuchulain was able to trace the Connachtmen by their tracks in the snow. After slaying the first Connacht scouts, Cuchulain again put the Connachtmen under the *geissa*; this time he drove four poles into the earth using only three fingers, and placed the heads of the slain Connacht scouts atop each. He again left a message. Fergus arrived on the scene and bade the Connachtmen to halt; they were again under *geissa*, and no advance could be made until someone was able to remove the pole with but three fingers. Fergus tried, and seventeen chariots broke beneath him before he was able to remove the poles. Fergus announced to the Connachtmen that Cuchulain had imposed these *geissa* to buy time until the Ulster warriors recovered from their illness.

Because Cuchulain's face was unknown to the Connachtmen except in the state caused by his battle frenzy, he was able to pass among them undetected. Cuchulain was walking in the

forest and came to the chariot driver of Oirlam, one of the
Connacht warriors; he demurely asked the chariot driver
whether he could lend a hand to repair the chariots. The
driver thanked him and said that Cuchulain could help with
trimming the chariot poles. Cuchulain grabbed the poles by
their tops and pulled off the branches with his toes, then
smoothed off the bark with his hands. When the chariot
driver returned, he marveled that the poles looked as if they
had been worked by a master. The charioteer asked Cuchulain
who he was, and when the hero said his name, the chariot
driver prepared to die. But Cuchulain told the driver that his
business was slaying warriors, not the unarmed. The chariot
driver ran to tell his master the story, and the entire camp of
Connachtmen was terrified.

Maeve's troops met Cuchulain, and the hero killed three of
them with but one stroke of his sword. The Connachtmen
knew that the battle was lost. Now Maeve sought to bribe
Cuchulain, and she sent Fergus MacRoy to negotiate. The
pact was made: instead of sending her entire army, Maeve
would now send one warrior at a time to fight against Cuchulain. She sought to send Fergus against Cuchulain, but both
refused as they were kinsmen.

In the meantime, Maeve seized the Brown Bull and took
him to County Armagh, a part of Ulster occupied by her
forces. Cuchulain slew Maeve's escorts, but failed to recapture
the bull, the greatest failure of his career.

The Connachtmen retreated to the south to regroup. The
Morrigan, a sorceress of great power, then came to Cuchulain
to seduce him. She sang his great exploits, praised his looks
and courage, and then offered herself to him. When he
refused, she vowed to destroy him.

Maeve sent Loch to do battle with Cuchulain, who was still a young man. Loch was an old warrior who had slain thousands; he was reluctant to take up arms against a hero so young. To fight Loch, Cuchulain stained his chin with blackberries in order for it to appear that he had a beard so that Loch would do battle with him. When the two were fighting, the spurned Morrigan came onto the field of battle disguised as a white heifer with red ears; Cuchulain wounded the "heifer's" eye when she opposed him. The Morrigan tried to attack him as a black eel as Cuchulain forded a stream while doing battle with Loch; she twisted herself around his leg and allowed Loch to land a blow that wounded Cuchulain. The Morrigan now took the form of a wolf and snarled at Cuchulain to distract him, allowing Loch to land still another blow. At this, Cuchulain was overtaken by the battle fury and drove the *Gae-bolga* against the Connacht champion. Dying, Loch asked Cuchulain to allow his body to fall on the Connacht side of the stream. With great respect for his foe, Cuchulain granted Loch's last wish.

The burden of killing so great a champion as Loch, indeed the whole issue of killing, wore heavily upon Cuchulain and he became very sad. He was angry that the men of Ulster were ill and that he had to do all the fighting, and he was weary of his many trials.

He cried aloud that he was tired "unto death." He decided to rest and lay at the burying ground at Learga, but he could not sleep lest the Connachtmen come by stealth and kill him. He was so sad that he began to lose his will not only to fight, but to live. The struggle wasn't worth it; he had the blood of great and brave heroes on his hands. He was so weary, however, that he could not help but sleep.

As his eyes became heavy, a tall and handsome warrior appeared to him, dressed in a golden tunic, bearing a long

black lance and pure silver shield, his face bathed in light. It
was Cuchulain's father, Lugh. Lugh spoke softly to his son,
saying, "Sleep, Cuchulain, for three days. I will myself take
your place in battle." As Cuchulain fell into a deep slumber,
Lugh applied healing herbs to his son's wounds. At the end of
the three days, Cuchulain awoke completely refreshed and
healed. Lugh had kept the enemy at bay, which made Maeve
all the more determined to see Cuchulain die at the hand of
his best friend.

Cuchulain and Ferdia

Cuchulain loved the warrior Ferdia as his own brother. The
two had learned the arts of war together as youths and were
known throughout the land as the greatest of all warriors;
cruel fate decreed that one would have to die at the hand of
the other.

Ferdia found himself in the service of Queen Maeve, and
she begged him many times to take up arms against Cuchulain; each time he refused. Then Maeve offered the hand of her
daughter Findabair if Ferdia would fight his old comrade. Still
Ferdia refused. Finally, Maeve accused Ferdia of cowardice,
vowing that all Ireland would ridicule him forever if he did
not fight Cuchulain. Maeve used magic to cause Ferdia to fall
in love with her daughter, and at long last, Ferdia relented.
Still, Ferdia was broken with sadness, and there was silence
throughout Maeve's camp.

In the morning, Ferdia went to the stream where Cuchulain
was encamped. Upon seeing his old friend approaching in a
war chariot, Cuchulain was astonished. For a brief moment,
he thought that Ferdia had left the service of Maeve to join
him in fighting for Ulster. One look at the grave look on

Ferdia's face, however, and he knew. "How can the friend of my youth do battle with me? Weren't we both the students of Sceatha? Didn't we play together in the forests? If we meet in battle, one of us will surely die."

Ferdia was unable to look directly at Cuchulain; it was too painful. Ferdia responded, "Yes, I am the same Ferdia. Don't think of our past relationship; just know that it was inevitable that we would do combat."

They agreed to do battle first with the javelins they used in their youth. They battled for hours, but so great was the skill of each warrior that neither was wounded. As the sun set, they agreed to stop fighting and embraced each other three times. Then each went to rest in his own camp.

They met again at dawn of the next day, and the two heroes fought again until dusk. Each had wounded the other, and both were weary of fighting. As a gesture of their past friendship, they sent each other healing herbs.

At dawn on the third day, they again met for battle. Ferdia summoned all of his valor and resolve and came to the field with a menacing scowl on his face. Cuchulain had placed spies in Maeve's court, and the previous night they informed him that Ferdia would gain the hand of Findabair through this fighting. Cuchulain was now sick with rage. "It is for a woman that you betray me? It is to buy your bride that you take up arms against a friend who loved you? Ferdia, prepare to die. Findabair was the price of your betrayal once; now death will be the price."

These words were more than Ferdia could bear. Both fought furiously, the fighting fueled by anger, betrayal, and battle fury. The two heroes were so equal a match that the combat was bloody and brutal, and horrible wounds were inflicted. That night, as they returned to their camp, no em-

braces were exchanged, no herbs were sent, and no kind remi-
niscences were spoken. Both knew that one of them would not
live to see the next dusk.

As dawn came, they wore their best, knowing that death
was in the air. Ferdia wore his silk tunic, a leather apron, and a
breastplate of granite (as Ferdia knew that Cuchulain would
use the *Gae-bolga* against him). Cuchulain also wore his best
battle dress. Cuchulain looked at the sky and saw that it was
the very color of blood. The red of dawn dissipated slowly,
much as blood falling into a stream, which Cuchulain took as a
portent. Cuchulain instructed Laeg, his charioteer, to taunt
him and mock him, so as to spur him to fight. Laeg responded,
"It has been your fate to die as the result of a woman, whether
Findabair or another."

Cuchulain was seized by the *riastradh*; the battle madness
blinded his heart and mind as his body contorted, to the point
of frightening Ferdia. At last, Cuchulain dealt the death blow
with the *Gae-bolga*, which he flung from Ferdia's toes into his
stomach; it shattered the granite breastplate into gravel.
Ferdia fell into the stream, and his spilling blood looked like
the dissipating dawn sky that morning. Ferdia looked up at
Cuchulain and cried, "It is a sad thing to die at your hands,
my bother." At this, Cuchulain regained his wits and emerged
from the *riastradh* to see his friend dying. He embraced
Ferdia one last time.

It was the custom of a warrior to behead his foe, but this
Cuchulain could not do, wishing to honor Ferdia. Instead he
wept and grieved. So stricken was Cuchulain that he went off
to a secret place to rest. The compassion of the Tuatha De
Danaan led them to cover his body with healing herbs to fight
another day. Three days later, he was again able to do battle
with the Connachtmen.

As a hero, Cuchulain was subject to the *geissa*, but he had undertaken so many that he could no longer keep one without breaking another. The *geissa* included not passing a hearth without eating the food; another *geissa* forbade the eating of dog meat. Once, three sorceresses of Maeve were roasting a dog over a fire, and Cuchulain broke one *geis* to keep another. Promptly, Cuchulain began to lose his powers.

After a series of battles, Cuchulain bound himself to a pillar, so that were he to die, he would die on his feet like a hero. The wicked Morrigan and her sisters took the form of ravens and called out to Cuchulain's enemies to behead the hero, which was done. And as is said at the end of an Irish tale, *Sin mar a bhfuil an scéal* (That's the story).

Connections

In the Cuchulain myth, one can readily identify the key elements common to myths of the hero. He is born of a divine father and a mortal mother, yet is raised by his faithful stepfather, Sualtam. His birth is miraculously accompanied by the portent, the birth of twin foals. Cuchulain shows prodigy by slaying the 350 boy-warriors sent by Conchobar, his uncle, who already sees the four-year-old as a rival. *Cuchulain* is the hero name taken by the boy Setanta. Like us, Cuchulain goes through peril and trials to gain wisdom and become a hero.

The story of Cuchulain and Connla is a poignant tale of the freedom and burden of human choice. By placing Connla under the *geis* of doing battle with every warrior the lad encounters, Cuchulain has made a choice to call his son to the heroic life. That very choice is a painful burden, as the *geis* results in Cuchulain slaying his own son.

Another interesting thing to note is that many of Cuchulain's battle opponents are women, a fact that Robert Graves and other scholars interpreted as the record of an ancient battle between matriarchy and an emerging patriarchy.

The two striking elements in the "Trials of Cuchulain" episodes are the sense of "the hero as every man"—to use Joseph Campbell's words—and the appearances of Lugh, the sun god.

Cuchulain assumes a rather ordinary appearance when he is not overtaken by the battle frenzy. This conveys that the hero myths are truly an eternal mirror in which we see ourselves. Most of the time, Cuchulain looks very much like any face in the crowd; he hardly appears heroic. Cuchulain is transformed, however, by heroic action.

In these stories, Lugh appears but twice. The first time, Lugh gives Cuchulain the wheel of light to guide him through the most dangerous phase of the journey to Sceatha's land. The second appearance of Lugh speaks to the appearance of the numinous in the dark moments of existence. Lugh appears now in the most tragic moment, when Cuchulain has lost the will to fight on, and Lugh is literally a light in the darkness. So it is in our own lives that during our most tragic moments we experience transcendence.

As we've seen earlier, betrayal by a friend or a brother is a common theme in the myths of the hero. The painful burden of Ferdia's choice to join Cuchulain's enemies leads to Ferdia's death and Cuchulain's subsequent sorrow and anguish.

Cuchulain's death is also caused by the burden of choice. Cuchulain, as we are, is faced with an ethical dilemma in complying with the *geissa*. One universal human tragedy is the sense of having to violate one promise, commitment, or commandment in order to comply with another. Choice in human existence is a paradox. The paradox of the conflicting *geissa* removes Cuchulain's invincibility in battle. It is the ethical dilemma, the burden of choice, that ultimately renders Cuchulain mortal; this is a potent statement on the human condition. We, too, live and die by our choices and the conflicting duties we must keep.

OKUNINUSHI
(Japan)

The source for the myth of Okuninushi is the *Kojiki*, or *Records of Ancient Matters*, the mythical history of Japan that covers the creation of the world to Japan's earliest emperors.

Okuninushi was the son of the storm god Susanowo, who had eighty other sons. While the other sons were as cruel and destructive as their father, Okuninushi took after his beautiful and gentle mortal mother, Kishinada. Okuninushi was always patient, humble, honest, and kind—and the most handsome of all Susanowo's sons.

The nasty brothers were terrible to Okuninushi, treating him worse than a servant and forcing him to carry the heavy loads of their possessions. All eighty brothers wanted to marry the Yakami-hime (*hime* means *princess*) of Inaba and incessantly quarreled among themselves as to who was the best suitor. The eighty brothers then set out on the road to Inaba to compete for winning the princess's hand. On the road, they encountered a poor hare who had lost all of its fur. The miserable creature was shivering, and the cruel brothers told the poor creature to first bathe in the sea, then run

quickly up to the peak of a mountain, where its fur would then
be restored.

The hare did as they told him. The salt of the sea burned
and dried out its bare skin, causing it to crack and bleed. Then
the hare ran quickly up a mountain, where the raw, bitter
winds made the pain even worse. Exhausted, the hare prepared to die on the mountaintop.

Okuninushi happened to be climbing that very mountain,
bearing a heavy pack of his brothers' possessions. Okuninushi
saw the poor hare, felt compassion, and approached it to help.
The hare saw the goodness in Okuninushi's eyes and cried
out, "Please help me! I am about to die!" Okuninushi asked
the hare what had happened.

So, the hare first told the story of how it had lost its fur. The
clever hare had once decided to cross a sea inlet, but had no
boat. So, it thought to use the crocodile. The hare said out
loud, "I wonder how many crocodiles there are in the sea and
whether there are more crocodiles in the sea than there are
hares on the land." This statement appealed to the pride of the
crocodiles, and they lined up across the inlet to show their
number. The hare then hopped across the inlet on the backs of
the crocodiles. Arrogantly, the hare said, just as it landed on
the last crocodile's back, "Stupid crocodiles, I really don't
care how many of you there are; I merely wanted to cross the
inlet." The last crocodile was angry at being used, and bit off
all of the hare's fur.

Okuninushi responded that it was wrong for the hare to
take advantage of the crocodiles and then insult them. But
while the hare deserved some punishment for its behavior,
there was no reason to further punish the poor creature.

The hare then told Okuninushi that its death was caused by
the action of the eighty brothers. Thinking of his siblings'

many indignities toward him, Okuninushi felt a deepening of his compassion. Okuninushi softly told the hare that it could win relief by bathing in a stream of fresh water and rolling in certain herbs that would soothe and heal the skin, allowing the fur to grow back richer than before. Knowing Okuninushi's kind nature, the hare did as his benefactor suggested.

Soon, the grateful hare hopped back to Okuninushi to show its new coat of luxurious fur and to thank his benefactor for his kindness. The hare said, "I have no riches, but I can tell the future. You, and not your brothers, will marry the princess and rule the land."

Meanwhile, the brothers had arrived at the court, where they tried and tried to impress the princess, but to no avail. She found them cruel, boorish, and childish. She had heard that there was yet another brother named Okuninushi, said to be the kindest and most handsome man in the realm. So, the princess announced that it was Okuninushi whom she wished to marry.

The eighty brothers were furious and vowed to kill Okuninushi. So, they found Okuninushi on the road and asked him to help them catch a wild red boar as they drove it down the mountain. However, the brothers had actually heated a boulder in the shape of a wild boar until it was red-hot. They then flung it down the mountain at Okuninushi, who burned to death. Yet the Celestial Ruling Deities will never allow such evil to triumph over good or allow the innocent to be exploited. When Kishinada, distraught at the death of her son, cried aloud to the Celestial Ruling Deities, they sent three *kami* messengers to revive Okuninushi.

With Okuninushi thus resurrected, the brothers were more determined than ever to kill him. So they seized him and crushed the life out of him under a large tree. But once more the Celestial Ruling Deities sent three *kami* to revive him. So Okuninushi rose again and went to see Susanowo at his palace in Yomi, the underworld realm of the dead, where Susanowo was consigned by Amaterasu.

When his cruel father saw him, Susanowo felt proud, but jealous of his son's bravery and favor with the Celestial Ruling Deities. So he wanted to put his son, and rival, Okuninushi, to the test. Susanowo had a beautiful daughter named Suseribime, Okuninushi's half sister. As in Greece, incest was forbidden to all but the gods and heroes; in ruling families, half brothers and half sisters were allowed to marry. Okuninushi and Suseribime fell in love and slept together. Susanowo knew this and set Okuninushi to three grueling tests, which Okuninushi had to pass before leaving Yomi.

The first night, Okuninushi was locked in a room full of poisonous vipers; the second night, the room was full of stinging centipedes and bees. But both nights he escaped with the help of Suseribime. This made Susanowo angry and more determined.

Susanowo challenged Okuninushi to fetch an arrow that the storm god shot into a grassy meadow. Okuninushi went into the grass to find the arrow, but Susanowo had dried the grass, then set it afire. The field mice who lived in the grass helped Okuninushi, by first retrieving the arrow and then showing him their holes in the cool earth, which led to safety.

Susanowo was now impressed with Okuninushi's courage and decided to go to take a nap. Okuninushi and Suseribime tied Susanowo's hair to the bed as he slept, then placed a large stone in front of the door, and fled Yomi for earth. When Susanowo awoke, he decided to pursue them. However, it took him so long to untangle his hair and move the stone that the couple were successful in their flight.

Okuninushi married both Suseribime and the Princess Yakami of Inaba, as well as many other wives, and produced great sons to rule the islands.

Connections

Japanese scholars have traditionally interpreted the struggles between Okuninushi and Susanowo (and, by extension, the eighty brothers) as a symbolic representation of the battle between civilization and barbarism in early Japanese society; this interpretation is the same that is provided for the story of Amaterasu and Susanowo (see page 112). With the rise of psychoanalysis, twentieth-century Japanese scholars have attributed the duality to the conflicting creative and destructive impulses in every human being. The Japanese also point out that Okuninushi is the first *Japanese* hero to appear in the *Kojiki*; he is not a god dwelling in the heavens or the underworld, but a man who lives on the earth. This is fitting, as it meets the needs of a myth of the finite hero, true of Okuninushi—the son of a divine father and a mortal mother— and all great heroes of the myths.

The cultural values in the story of Okuninushi need to be contrasted with those of Cuchulain and Theseus. Whereas the Irish and Greek heroes are introduced to us in battles, the first trait demonstrated by the Japanese hero is compassion, which is characteristic of the Japanese love of nature.

Okuninushi, like Theseus, descends to the underworld, where he is exposed to great trials. And much like Theseus and ourselves, it is love that guides him safely through the perils and leads him back to the world of the living. Love, once again, is stronger than death.

THE STORY OF QUETZALCOATL: THE HERO BECOMES A GOD
(Mexico)

Quetzalcoatl was many things: (1) a historical personage—a great priest-king and religious reformer who lived in approximately the tenth century A.D. (We know that a Toltec prince named Tonantzin was forced to leave Tula because of his opposition to human sacrifice and went to Chichén Itzá, where he ruled the Maya as Kulkulcán/Quetzalcoatl); (2) a god of the winds, the sun, and the planet Venus; (3) the cultural hero and expected "messiah" of the pre-Columbian Mexicans; and (4) a god-hero who served as patron of the arts, writing, and the cultivation of maize. These identities became fused together over time.

All of our modern retellings of the story of Quetzalcoatl owe their thanks to one great source, *Historia general de las cosas de Nueva España*, written by the Spanish priest Sahagún, who laboriously recorded the Aztec myths just as Catholic missionaries destroyed almost all the sacred books (codices) that formed the canons of sacred history. The chronicler of the Maya, Bishop de Landa, performed a similar task of recording the myths of the Yucatán Maya.

The Birth of Quetzalcoatl

There are several stories regarding the birth of Quetzalcoatl. One version has him born of a virgin named Chimalman, to whom the supreme god, Onteotl (the Great Father-Mother) appeared in a dream. Onteotl showed his/her face to Chimalman and her two sisters. The two sisters died instantly from the gaze, but Chimalman, pure of heart, survived and conceived a son, Quetzalcoatl. In another version, the virgin Chimalman swallows a sacred piece of jade and conceives Quetzalcoatl.

A third story of Quetzalcoatl's birth is directly tied to his identity as a deity of the sun and planet Venus. In this story, Quetzalcoatl is the son of a mother who already has four thousand children who have left her and now form the stars of the Milky Way. This mother was saddened to be alone and have her children so far from her bosom. She began to weep from longing. Onteotl took pity on her in her loneliness and caused a feather of the sacred quetzal bird to drift down to her from the sky. She put the feather close to her heart, then she began sweeping the heavens with the feather to gather her children together. But the children were so dispersed that her sweeping proved futile. But the feather was the means by which Onteotl impregnated the woman, and she gave birth to Quetzalcoatl, the greatest of her children, as well as his dark twin brother, Tezcatlipoca. And wouldn't Quetzalcoatl appear to be greater than the many stars? Don't the stars of night flee when the planet Venus appears as morning star and then "becomes" the sun?

A fourth version of Quetzalcoatl's birth concerns some point in the early history of the Aztecs, when a barbaric people known as the Chichimecas fought the Toltecs for control of the Valley of Mexico. The battle between the Chichimecas and Toltecs was the struggle between barbarism and civilization. The Toltecs, led by the great chief Mixcoatl, managed to take possession of vast areas of Mexico.

There was a brave woman named Chimalman who put on the disguise of a warrior and went to visit Mixcoatl, with whom she had fallen in love. She then took off her disguise and stood naked before the great leader. Mixcoatl at first thought Chimalman to be a spy from the Chichimecas, sent to seduce and kill him, so he shot four arrows at her body. Three of the arrows struck her, but did not injure her. The fourth arrow pierced her womb, and nine months later she gave birth to a child named Quetzalcoatl, after the Toltec god of culture, the winds, and the sun. Other sources tell us that she gave her son the name Tonantzin and that he assumed the name Quetzalcoatl upon becoming the priest-king of the Toltecs. Chimalman died in childbirth, and the boy was sent to be raised by priests and wise men. Mixcoatl was slain through treachery, and mutiny and destiny ordained that his son would regain the Toltec throne and lead the people into a golden age.

Thus, it appears, the identities of the mythic hero Quetzalcoatl and the Toltec god became blurred, confusing both the ancient Mexicans and readers of the myths today.

The Reign and Trials of Quetzalcoatl

The reign of Quetzalcoatl was a golden age. The king himself taught the people how to use metals, grow new and better crops, create great works of art, and operate an efficient government. It is said that ears of maize grew so large that a worker could carry only one at a time, and that the cotton grew already dyed in brilliant colors. The people remembered Quetzalcoatl's rule as the "golden age of Anáhuac."

However, as soon as Quetzalcoatl became the ruler of the Toltecs, his "dark brother," Tezcatlipoca, began plotting his overthrow. While Quetzalcoatl was creative and constructive— for example, he was even credited with bringing maize back from the underworld—Tezcatlipoca is his opposite number, a force of anarchy and destruction. And since so much of Quetzalcoatl's authority to rule was based on his moral authority, Tezcatlipoca sought to bring Quetzalcoatl to shame.

Tezcatlipoca first took on the appearance of a crooked old man and offered Quetzalcoatl a drink of intoxicating liquor with the assurance that the drink would lift anxiety and remove all concerns about death. Because Quetzalcoatl was growing older, he took a drink (which was pulque, from which tequila is distilled, and is still drunk in Mexico today). He then asked Tezcatlipoca where he should go to regain his youth. The evil brother directed him to a place called Tollantapantla, where an old man would be waiting for him. The old man would direct him to a fountain of youth.

With Quetzalcoatl off in Tollantapantla, Tezcatlipoca sought to bring shame on the priest-king through Quetzalcoatl's daughter. Tezcatlipoca then assumed the guise of an extremely handsome youth—a young chile seller who appeared, virtually naked, in the marketplace where the princess was certain to walk. The "chile seller" then approached the princess and flirted with her. One glance at the "chile seller" and the princess was so smitten that she became sick with desire. (*Chile* today is still Mexican slang for *penis*.)

When the princess returned to the palace, she was overcome with love sickness, languishing and moping about to the point that Quetzalcoatl, upon his return, demanded an explanation. When his daughter told the story of the young chile seller, the priest-king was outraged, instantly suspecting Tezcatlipoca of using a charm, but also angry that a naked young chile seller had the impertinence to approach his daughter.

Quetzalcoatl sent his servants out to find the chile seller, who suddenly appeared just as they were about to give up their search. They seized him and brought him before Quetzalcoatl, who lectured him on his lack of modesty, impertinence, and vulgarity. The captive chile seller explained that he came from a country where people seldom wore any clothes. Quetzalcoatl then ordered his servants to bathe and clothe the chile seller. For despite serious reservations, Quetzalcoatl knew that there would be no peace in his home until his daughter married the chile seller.

Tezcatlipoca's plan was working perfectly; he had schemed his way right into Quetzalcoatl's household, even into the princess's bed. And when the Toltecs learned that Quetzalcoatl had given his daughter's hand to an obscure chile seller from some distant land, they were outraged that this stranger had been chosen over all of the noble and worthy young warriors of the land. Now Tezcatlipoca had sown discord even within Quetzalcoatl's armies.

After a time, it became apparent to Quetzalcoatl exactly who his son-in-law was, but by then it was too late. Tezcatlipoca had organized a band of rebel troops against Quetzalcoatl's Toltec warriors. After a series of defeats at the hands of the rebels, Quetzalcoatl had no choice but to reach terms with his son-in-law. But Tezcatlipoca was not satisfied with military victory alone: he now schemed to wreck Toltec society. And he still wanted to shame Quetzalcoatl.

Once, Tezcatlipoca cast a spell on the Toltecs that caused them to begin singing until they turned to stone. Another time, Tezcatlipoca reassumed the body of the chile seller and appeared in the marketplace, where he made a crude puppet of Quetzalcoatl dance in his hand. The loyal Toltecs were outraged by this insult to their ruler and stoned Tezcatlipoca to death—or so it appeared. (As Tezcatlipoca was a god, he had merely cast off the chile seller's body.) The body decomposed and a plague followed; wherever the winds carried the stench, multitudes of Toltecs died. To stop the plague, the Toltecs tied ropes to the corpse to move it away, but despite the combined strength of hundreds of warriors, the corpse could not be moved. Thus, the plague continued.

Tezcatlipoca then tried to destroy Toltec society by causing a volcanic eruption that rained burning rocks on them, killing hundreds and destroying the crops of the survivors.

Tezcatlipoca had succeeded in bringing destruction to the land and people, but he had not yet brought shame on Quetzalcoatl—the one thing necessary to complete the destruction of his rival.

Tezcatlipoca went to Quetzalcoatl under the pretense of making peace. During their meeting, Tezcatlipoca (the name means *smoking mirror*) pulled out a mirror, and Quetzalcoatl was shocked to see how old he had become. Tezcatlipoca offered Quetzalcoatl an intoxicating drink that would restore his youth. The wary Quetzalcoatl at first merely dipped his finger in the cup and applied a few drops to his lips. The potion was so strong, however, that Quetzalcoatl lost control of his senses and drank the entire cup, collapsing on the floor.

Shortly after, the high priestess came upon Quetzalcoatl, saw the pitcher of potion, and drank the remains. The two remained collapsed for two days and neglected all of the rituals necessary to the people's welfare.

When Quetzalcoatl finally awoke, he couldn't remember anything that had happened since Tezcatlipoca had shown him the mirror. With the priestess lying next to him, he wondered whether he had violated her chastity; worse still, as he was a priest, the priestess was referred to as his sister, and this would be a ritual "incest," the penalty for which was death.

As soon as Quetzalcoatl's head had cleared, he was filled

with shame. His face was bloated from his drunkenness, and he donned a jade mask to hide his face, and his embarrassment, from the people. Quetzalcoatl then called all of his servants together, telling them that his great sin required that he leave his people. He ordered them to build him a tomb and throw his vast treasures into the canyons and rivers. (To this day, that is where people find gold and silver.)

Quetzalcoatl remained in his tomb for three nights, and then he returned to his people, telling them that he would go to the land of fire and death.

On his way to the Eastern Sea (the Atlantic), Quetzalcoatl made an arrow from the *pachotl* tree and shot this arrow into another tree, forming a cross. This became an emblem of Quetzalcoatl and was to be the sign by which the people would know his return.

At the Eastern Sea, Quetzalcoatl prophesied that he would leave on his raft of serpents, but would return in the year One Reed, which occurs only once every fifty-two years. (The Mayans had the same story for Kulkulcán.) The bearded, fair-skinned Quetzalcoatl, with the cross as his emblem, was expected to return in such a year . . . and was believed to have done so, in the European year 1519. Again, myth here has a profound impact on actual historical events.

In that year, fair-skinned, bearded men arrived, bearing crosses. To their vast surprise, they were not only met with minimal resistance, but welcomed. The strangers also bore banners with the golden lion of Castile on it; certainly, this looked like the jaguar emblem of the long-awaited Quetzalcoatl.

One of those strangers, the Spaniard Bernal Diaz (1492–1591) wrote that the Aztec Emperor Moctezuma (given below as "Montezuma") met the Spaniards with joy and great hospitality.

Then Montezuma began a very good speech, saying that he was delighted to have such valiant gentlemen as Cortés and the rest of us in his home and in his kingdom. He said he would share all that he possessed with us. He ended by saying that we must truly be the men about whom his ancestors had long ago prophesied, saying that they would come from the direction of the sunrise to rule over these lands.

Was this the return of Quetzalcoatl—or was it Tezcatlipoca's cruelest trick? The Aztec details of the return of Quetzalcoatl had him coming from the east, riding a deer (the Aztecs did not know horses until the arrival of the Spaniards), wearing spurs, and bearing the cross and jaguar emblems.

Connections

The Quetzalcoatl myth is a typical myth of the hero, in terms of the elements of the miraculous circumstances of his conception and birth; the trials; the "journey to the underworld" (his remaining in his tomb for three days); and other elements.

In the four different stories surrounding his birth, the origin of the deity Quetzalcoatl, the cultural hero, and the priest-king are all set forth. The one story has him sired by Onteotl, the Great Father-Mother, and clearly establishes Quetzalcoatl's cosmic origin with the story of sweeping the stars.

The name *Quetzalcoatl* is an Aztec (or more correctly, Nahua) name meaning *plumed serpent*; his Mayan name *Kulkulcán* has the same meaning. The name speaks to the human condition of identity within the cosmos. Quetzalcoatl is the fusion of elements that indicate the earth, underworld (serpent), and heaven (bird).

The heroic struggle centers around the contest between Quetzalcoatl and his dark twin, Tezcatlipoca. On an obvious level, it is a depiction of the struggle between the forces of creation and destruction (as in the Japanese myths we have read), as well as the struggle of those forces within every human being. The duality, the sense of Quetzalcoatl as "twin," is central to the meaning of this myth. It makes a statement regarding the human condition and the Mexican worldview of *difrasmo*, wherein truth was always to be found in paradox and dualities. C. A. Burland, a scholar of Mesoamerican mythology, attributes this linguistic meaning:

> Among the Aztecs, it [the name Quetzalcoatl] carried the inner meaning of "The Most Precious Twin," since *quetzal* was loosely used as a term for precious and beautiful things, and *coatl* meant "twin." The allusion was to the nature of the planet Venus in its aspects of Morning and Evening Star. Of these two, the Morning Star was the Quetzal or "precious one."

Another aspect of the "twin" nature of Quetzalcoatl is as both Venus and sun god; to the ancient Mexicans, the morning star (Venus) appeared to metamorphose into the sun.

This myth speaks to the human condition; it is necessary for Quetzalcoatl and every other hero to pass through the underworld. Each of us has passed, or will pass at some time, through an underworld of the "dark night of the soul," engendered through defeat, frustration, loss, or other of the tragedies that invade each life. But there is more in Quetzalcoatl's passage.

His passage through the underworld (for three days, like Jesus and Cuchulain) takes place after Tezcatlipoca has arranged the greatest possible shame for a priest-king—ritual incest—and ends Quetzalcoatl's reign. This episode speaks to the human conditions of choice and finitude. For it is out of fear of his own finitude—even vanity—that Quetzalcoatl becomes vulnerable to Tezcatlipoca; the onset of aging wrought the choice that cost Quetzalcoatl his throne. This bears a powerful lesson of the consequences of one failing to accept one's finitude.

ODIN AND THOR: HEROIC GODS
(Norse)

Unlike the gods of other cultures, the Norse gods are under a death sentence. The Norse gods, like us, are finite. They are only temporarily immortal. Consequently, they act much as heroes, even if they are gods.

Our sources for the Norse myths are the Icelandic sagas.

Odin Pays the Price for Wisdom

Odin was Thor's father and the wisest of the gods. He acquired great wisdom—but only at a great cost. To drink at the well of wisdom, Odin bartered one of his eyes. Once Odin had drunk of the well, he also learned that he was finite and doomed: the day of the Twilight of the Gods would come, and he and all the lords of Asgard, land of the gods, would be annihilated.

Then, there is the story of how Odin obtained the Mead of Inspiration. Often Odin assumed the form of an eagle and circled the earth just to see what was going on in his realm. On one such journey, Odin learned that dwarfs had killed the giant Kvasnir, mixed the giant's blood with honey, and fermented it into three barrels of a wondrous mead that gave inspiration to the drinker.

The same group of dwarfs had killed the parents of a giant named Suttung. The angry Suttung took vengeance by seizing the dwarfs, placing them on a rock during a low tide, and then leaving them to drown as the high tide came. In order to buy their survival, the dwarfs told Suttung that they possessed the Mead of Inspiration, which would be forever lost were they to perish. Odin knew that he had to obtain this mead for the gods and not allow it to fall into the hands of their enemies, the giants.

So Odin joined the forces of Baugi, Suttung's brother, as they were harvesting grain. As the nine men were cutting the sheaves, Odin appeared with a magic whetstone to sharpen the sickles. The whetstone was so wonderful that the nine began quarreling over it and finally killed each other. Odin then pledged to Baugi, the god of poetry, that he himself would finish the harvest, doing the work of nine men in exchange for the Mead of Inspiration.

So Baugi described how Suttung had secreted the mead deep within the rocks of the earth. Baugi then drilled a hole into the rock, and Odin, taking the form of a serpent, slithered down into the fissure. There he found one of Suttung's daughters standing guard over the mead. He spent three nights with her, and each night he took one draft of mead that was sufficient to empty one barrel completely. After he had drunk all three barrels, Odin slithered back out through the rock, assumed the form of an eagle, and flew back to Asgard, where he spat the mead into the drinking vessels of the gods.

Another time, Odin fasted by hanging himself on Yggdrasil, the World Tree; for nine days and nights he hung there, pierced by a spear. He did this to make a sacrifice to himself, for men were hung on trees and speared as offerings to Odin. At the end of the nine days, Odin looked below him and discovered the mystery of the runes.

Thor and the Giant of Utgardloki

Thor, god of thunder, is not invincible; he was once vanquished by a giant. Once, Loki, the trickster god, and Thor set out on a journey, accompanied by two young attendants. They wandered and wandered through a vast, dense forest, never seeing even one house. When they were thoroughly exhausted, they at last spied a house with a large, oval door. They went inside and fell sound asleep.

In the middle of the night, they were disturbed by strange roars; they felt as if caught in an earthquake, for the floors shook in rhythm with the roars. Once awake, they couldn't go back to sleep and cowered in a corner with Thor holding his hammer at the ready. There they stood in terror until the dawn came.

At daylight, they ventured out of the house only to find a huge giant, Skrymir, sound asleep. The roaring that they had heard through the night was Skrymir's snoring. The giant was so huge that Thor even wondered whether his magic hammer, gloves, and belt would be adequate to defend them from this monster. Skrymir was roused by the sound of Thor preparing for battle by fastening his enchanted belt.

To the surprise of the travelers, Skrymir was friendly to them and invited them to go with him on his daily rounds. As the giants were sworn enemies of the gods, Thor was reluctant to trust any of them, let alone Skrymir.

At night, Skrymir decided to rest beneath an oak, but first the giant asked Thor to prepare their dinner. Thor used all of his might to loosen the cords on the bag that Skrymir said contained food, but to no avail. While Thor was struggling, Skrymir fell sound asleep. Eager to claim another victory over a giant to brag about, Thor seized his hammer and dealt a massive blow to Skrymir's head. The giant woke up and said, "An acorn must have fallen on my head!" When Skrymir again fell asleep, Thor once more struck the giant with his mighty hammer. Skrymir again woke up to say, "A twig must have fallen on my head!" Then, with total concentration, Thor again struck Skrymir so hard that it had to do some damage. But, it did not. Instead, Skrymir rose and said, "A bird must have flown by and left droppings on my head!" The next morning, Skrymir took his leave of the travelers and told them that he was going to Utgard, where giants even greater than he dwelled. But Thor and his party, seeking glory, followed the giant's huge footprints.

Before long, the travelers came to Utgard, where the gates were so large that they slipped in easily between the bars of the gate. Utgardloki, king of Utgard and the giant king, taunted them into giving performances of their alleged prowess. One of the four travelers, the attendant boy Thjalfi, was the swiftest of men; he challenged a giant to a footrace. Of course, the giant's huge strides left Thjalfi far behind, and the assembled court roared with laughter. Loki was challenged to an eating contest, and he, too, was easily defeated by a giant.

Thor, never one to be reticent about his abilities, began to boast of his prowess as warrior and drinker. The giants brought out a huge drinking horn, and Thor began to take huge gulps from it. But the drinking horn always remained full! Thor again boasted of his strength and heroic exploits, and Utgardloki taunted Thor to pick up his old gray cat. As Thor's face grew red and he heaved a mighty grunt, he was only able to lift one of the cat's paws. Utgardloki then challenged Thor to wrestle an old, frail-looking giant woman, and she easily defeated him!

Humiliated and dismayed, the gods were escorted to the gate by Utgardloki himself. Utgardloki explained that he was actually Skrymir the giant and all of these tests were designed to teach the gods and their attendants wisdom. The giant had cast a spell over them that made things seem to be what they actually were not.

The sack containing food could not be opened by Thor, as the cords were not made of twine, but of double bands of iron. The head of the giant that Thor had thrice struck with all his might was actually a mountain. The champion who defeated Loki in the eating contest was fire, which consumes all things. The drinking horn that Thor could not empty had one of its ends in the sea, which would never go dry. The old gray cat was the Serpent of Midgard. The old woman who wrestled Thor was Old Age, which overcomes even the strongest. Thor, Loki, and the attendants returned home, much wiser than before.

Connections

The Norse gods are included in our chapter on heroes, as they are heroic gods. Unlike the gods of other cultures, the Norse gods are under a death sentence—and they are aware of this. They are finite, as their reign and existence is as sure to come to an end as are our own lives. Consequently, they act much like heroes. Like the heroes of other cultures and like us, Norse gods struggle for their existence and have to pay a high price for wisdom and inspiration. Unlike the gods of other cultures, these qualities are not inherently theirs.

Odin acquired his wisdom by bartering an eye, and the core of that wisdom was the knowledge of his finitude. There are two statements on the human condition here: First, the wise do not see as we do, and second, accepting and understanding one's finitude is the essence of wisdom.

The Mead of Inspiration does not belong to the gods, and so it, too, must be won by Odin at a great cost. But inspiration was not to be found in heaven, but rather on earth, and thus it must be brought to the gods in heaven. Humankind's struggle for inspiration is mirrored in this exploit; it is not ours, but must be acquired through struggle.

The episode of Thor and the giant Utgardloki is again a statement on the finitude of the gods and the costs of wisdom. The gods of Asgard are not only finite and destined to perish, their rule of the universe is constantly contested by a race of giants. For this reason again, they merit special treatment as heroic gods. And this episode with Thor speaks to our process of becoming. Thor uses his magic weapons and still no injury is inflicted on the giant Skrymir; we can often use the best tools we have and still fail to vanquish the many "giants" that threaten our existence. Moreover, it is by wrestling with truth, struggling against obstacles, running the race of life, and losing the contest that Thor and his companions gain wisdom. And the wisdom they gain is about finitude: They learn that their perception was faulty, that things are not as they seem. Likewise, only after wrestling with truths, abandoning our facile perceptions, and being defeated do we see things as they really are and gain wisdom. This is *our* story, as we struggle not merely for our existence itself, but for the wisdom to find meaning in it. One wrestles with truth.

* * *

As the myths of the hero speak to us about our personal struggles, finitude, process of becoming, and individual identity in the cosmos, there are other heroic myths that speak to our identity as nations or peoples. And these myths, too, speak in the language of tragedy and heroism. These are the foundation myths that create and sustain nations.

5. Foundation Myths

The Mexican author Carlos Fuentes once wrote that "Myth is a past with a future, exercising itself in the present." Nowhere is that more true than in foundation myths. Foundation, or civic, myths are the stories of the birth of nations or states. The foundation myth, set in the distant past, tells us what the character of the state is today and often prophesies future greatness.

The transition from the myths of the hero (in the previous chapter) to foundation myths (in this chapter) is a natural progression. For, as we will see, there are numerous hero myths that also work as foundation myths, in that the hero's quest is to found a nation or state. Also, as hero myths are about *individual* identity, so foundation myths are heroic stories of *collective* identity. The character of the founder is often reflected in the character of the state. The legitimacy of the state is predicated on the divine and royal lineage of the hero, who is also the ancestor of the ruling family.

The key elements to look for in the myths that follow are how foundation myths demonstrate what a people think of themselves. They demonstrate the divine basis for legitimacy of the state and provide a union between the divine and the nation's soil. Lastly, foundation myths give birth to collective symbols of identity, many of which we still recognize today as images of an entire nation.

THE FIRST EMPERORS
(Imperial China)

The Chinese call their country Zhongguo, or the Middle Kingdom, as they believe it to be the center of the world, the source of civilization, and the scene of the creation of the world. This myth reflects the Chinese pride in cultural and technological achievement, which began in the earliest days of the nation's mythical history.

The emperor is the Son of Heaven, as he is the descendant of the Three Celestial Sovereigns who first ruled China and developed the tools of civilization.

The first emperor was the great Fuxi, a divine being who was half-human and half-serpent. One story tells us that he sprang forth from a mountainside with his head covered with leaves. It is Fuxi who established the first Chinese civilization. He organized the empire by teaching people how to hunt, fish, and domesticate animals. Together with his wife (and sister) Niugua, he instituted marriage; Niugua is still considered the goddess of marriage.

The second emperor was their son, Xiannong, who was a reversed Minotaur, a being with the head of a bull and the body of a human being. He presided over the natural progression of the people from hunting, fishing, and herding to agriculture. So, Xiannong invented the wheel, the plow, and the ox yoke, teaching people how to prepare the fields for planting by burning and to use manure as fertilizer. About this time, illness came into the world, so Xiannong wrote a catalog of medicinal herbs; the herbs are still used for these purposes today.

Wangdi (or Huang Ti), the son of Xiannong by a mortal woman, was the third emperor and the first human ruler of China. He is known as the Yellow Emperor because he was born on Earth Element Day, symbolized by the color yellow. With herding and agriculture in place, Wangdi saw that it was now time to create cities and commerce. Wangdi accordingly invented mathematics, the calendar, astrology, and astronomy, built the first imperial palace, began the cultivation of bamboo, and established the first laws. It is Wangdi who made the first offerings to heaven. With the basics of civilization in place, Wangdi set out to refine the life of the Chinese by creating the first tools, pottery, musical instruments, canals, compasses, and roads. He is also remembered as the inventor of chopsticks. His wife, Xannu (whose name means *Silk Lady*), began the cultivation of silkworms and invented weaving.

With China thus civilized, barbarians came from all over the world to marvel at the emperor's realm. They wondered at the many inventions and high state of culture and went home to imitate the Chinese, spreading culture and technology throughout the world.

Connections

This relatively simple myth is a perfect place to begin, as it presents the essentials of the foundation myths in a straightforward manner. The divine ancestor, from whom the legitimate future rulers would be descended, is identified, and as one version has him springing forth from the mountainside, there is a connection made between heaven and the sacred soil of the nation.

The story also is very clear with regard to how China sees itself as the fountain of civilization, whence "barbarians" learned the basic elements of human culture. The particular Chinese character can be seen in the inventions of the early emperors and their wives: in addition to the usual implements of civilization, the Chinese founding deities offer us chopsticks, bamboo, and the art of silk cultivation, all of which are still readily recognized throughout the world as Chinese arts.

TANGUN
(Korea)

The rich mythology of Korea is, unfortunately, not widely known in the West. Korean mythology has its roots in the shamanism common to the Tungus peoples of Siberia, the Manchu, and probably the Ainu minority in Japan. However, the Korean peninsula's role as a crossroads of culture is reflected in commonalities with Chinese and Japanese mythology. Many historians postulate large migrations from Korea to Japan in ancient times.

This foundation myth bears a strong resemblance to that of China, yet the role of the bear and animal clans are more characteristic of Siberia.

Before the creation of humans, the Divine Being, Hwanin, ruled the universe with the help of wind, cloud, rain, and 360 other deities, so that each deity was responsible for one day of the year, with one vacation day. Hwanin's son, Hwanung, called the Son of Heaven, descended to the earth near present-day Seoul one day and went in search of a wife. Two creatures approached him, a bear and a tiger, both offering to marry him if he would transform them into human beings. So Hwanung gathered some magical herbs and placed them before the two animals, but only the bear ate them and was transformed into a beautiful woman. Hwanung married the bear-woman, and they produced a son, Tangun, who was the first shaman.

Tangun walked through the land, changing animals into people, and then organized them into tribes based on the animals they had formerly been. Thus, the earliest clans were the Dragon, Horse, Crane, Deer, and Egret. The tribes were grateful for the gift of humanity and vowed to serve Tangun in gratitude. In the western year 2333 B.C., Tangun established an altar to the Three Great Reverences—Heaven, Earth, and the Ancestors—and proclaimed the founding of the Kingdom of Chosŏn, Koryu, Korea.

Through Tangun, the son of the Son of Heaven, the Korean kings claimed a portion of divinity. The reverence toward Heaven thus meant loyalty to the king. The reverence to Earth was reverence to the bear-woman as mother of the kings, and the reverence to the Ancestors recalled the creation of the people from animals. Tangun's kingdom was great and his armies invincible. All non-Christian Koreans believe that when a shaman speaks, it is actually Tangun speaking through him or her.

Connections

The Korean founding myth reminds us again that in the myth of the hero, the hero, or the founder, is the child of a god and a mortal—in this case, a she-bear transformed into a mortal woman. Here, too, there is the connection between the divine and the nation's soil; we know exactly where in Korea the divine founder is said to have descended. Much as the hero myths speak to human finitude and identity, the foundation myths speak to the collective identity of a people relative to both a divine founder and the land in which they live.

The she-bear is an important totemic symbol, not only in ancient Korea, but of the Tungus, the Manchu, the Ainu of Japan, and the Algonquin and Pacific Northwest natives of our own continent. There is even evidence of bear cults in Paleolithic Europe. Why this fascination with the bear, and what connection does it have to this foundation myth?

In all these cultures, the veneration of the bear derived from the vague resemblance between the standing bear and the human form; the symbolic death and resurrection inherent in the bear's hibernation; the courage and ferocity of the she-bear in guarding her cubs; and the animal's incredible strength. Much as the Ainu of Japan ate bear meat in order to acquire these qualities, the ancient Koreans saw the legitimacy of their kings in divine ancestry matched with the noble character and bravery of the sacred bear; this connection passed by descent from the mother, who had been changed from a bear into a human being, on to the royal bloodline.

BHARATA
(India)

The name of India in Hindi and Sanskrit is Bharat and the Indian national epic is the *Mahabharata*, which is a play on words meaning either *Great India* or *Great Bharata*. This name honors the mythical founder of the Indian kingdom and the ancestor of the nation's mythic heroes.

There once lived a powerful king named Dushyanta, who ruled an area so vast that four seas touched its shores.

One day Dushyanta decided to go hunting in the forests at the foot of the Himalayas. After he had passed deep into the forest, Dushyanta came upon an ashram, the humble hermitage of a holy man, or *rishi*. Dushyanta was overcome by the beauty that surrounded the simple hut. The holiness of the hut's inhabitant was so great that the songs of the surrounding birds resembled hymns. Instead of their usual chattering, the monkeys recited holy mantras. The flowers nearby were more fragrant than any on earth. Tame bears and tigers slept beneath trees laden with fruit, and although Dushyanta was hunting, he knew to kill them would be sacrilege. On approaching the hut, Dushyanta ordered his servants to remain behind so that he could meet privately with the holy man.

There was no one to be found on the grounds of the ashram, so Dushyanta peered inside the door. Inside was the most beautiful girl he had ever seen, gracefully moving around the room serving tea to a visiting Brahman.

Dushyanta could hardly believe that such a beauty would be found in the home of a *rishi*. After all, holy men generally take such a strict vow of chastity that some are not even allowed to speak to women, let alone have one living under the same roof. So the king asked the maiden, "What is this place?"

The girl lowered her beautiful dark eyes and softly replied that this was the home of the great *rishi* Kanva and that she was his daughter. So great was Kanva's reputation that

Dushyanta readily recognized the name, but he was still very confused that such an extreme ascetic would have a child.

The girl, being possessed of great modesty, then told Dushyanta that the visiting Brahman would explain it all, as she could see in Dushyanta's eyes that he was more than merely curious about her. She demurely lowered her eyes and sat down.

The Brahman explained that there had once been a great yogi named Vishvamitra, who had ruled as a king but had abdicated his throne in order to follow a severe spiritual discipline that included chastity. His austerity and devotion were so great that he had developed great supernatural powers. As time went on, the spiritual strength of Vishvamitra became so vast that Indra, god of the heavens, feared that the sage could take the realm of heaven away from him simply by willing it. Knowing that chastity was a source of Vishvamitra's strength, Indra called the beautiful *apsaras* (heavenly dancing girl) Menaka and sent her to seduce Vishvamitra, thereby stripping the sage of his powers. Indra sent the gods Hawa (wind) and Kama (sexual desire) to assist Menaka in her mission.

Menaka went to the ashram of Vishvamitra, and the sage was so taken by her beautiful face that he was stunned out of his deep meditation. Just as Vishvamitra began to compose himself, Hawa sent a gust that lifted Menaka's robes, revealing a beautiful and sensuous body. At that, Kama shot one of his arrows directly into Vishvamitra's heart, and the sage could no longer contain himself. He immediately made love to Menaka, lost his powers, and was discredited as a *rishi*.

Menaka soon found herself pregnant. She could not return to the heavens, however, until she had delivered her half-mortal child. So, Menaka journeyed into the deep woods at the foot of the Himalayas and gave birth to a baby girl, charging the little *shakanta* birds to protect her. The sage Kanva found the baby, named her Shakuntala after the birds, and raised her as his own daughter. "And," said the Brahman, "this is Shakuntala."

Dushyanta was so smitten with Shakuntala that he immediately proposed marriage. Shakuntala at first refused, saying that she could not give her consent without the blessing of Kanva, her foster father, a man so holy that he was able to see into Dushyanta's heart and know his true intentions—which as we will see, were not entirely honest. This fact was not lost on Dushyanta, who wished to avoid this scrutiny. So the king begged Shakuntala to marry him, and she agreed on the condition that, were they to have a son, their child would be the sole heir to Dushyanta's throne, to which the love-struck king readily agreed. The Brahman pronounced the wedding vows, the newlyweds spent the night together in the forest, and Dushyanta took his leave so that she could inform Kanva of the news in private. He vowed to return for her in a few days.

When Kanva returned, Shakuntala was worried about his reaction to her marriage. When she told Kanva and explained the promise that Dushyanta had made, the old man replied that he already knew all about it. Kanva informed her that she was now pregnant with a child who would be so great that he would be an emperor who ruled kings, and that an entire nation would be named for him. He cryptically added that the world would recognize her son before his own father did. Shakuntala was so inspired by the first part of the prophecy that she never inquired about the meaning of the second part.

But the meaning became painfully clear after days, weeks, months, and then years passed without a word from Dushyanta. Shakuntala had given birth to a little boy who obviously had the blessings of the gods. As he walked through the forests, not only did the wild beasts leave him unharmed, they saluted him as their master. This began before the little boy even learned to walk, so Kanva named him All-Tamer.

Shakuntala was sad that Dushyanta had never returned or met his own son, so she spoke to Kanva, who told her, "It is too bad I was not here to meet Dushyanta in order to read the intentions of his heart." The old Brahman who had pronounced the wedding vows was now dead, so there was not one man who could witness that Shakuntala was Dushyanta's wife and All-Tamer the heir to the throne. Kanva finally told Shakuntala to go with her son and an escort of holy men to Dushyanta's court.

When the entourage arrived, the courtiers ran to Dushyanta and told him, "There is a poor woman here with a child who says that she is your wife and that the child is your heir!" Dushyanta flew into a rage and refused to see them. But Dushyanta's advisers warned him that the woman and boy were escorted by holy men, and if the king refused to see the visitors, Dushyanta risked offending the gods. So, Dushyanta relented, and Shakuntala and All-Tamer were conducted into his throne room.

Of course, Dushyanta immediately recognized Shakuntala, and the child resembled him greatly, but as the two visitors were dressed in the simple clothing of holy hermits, they hardly looked like a queen and a prince. Shakuntala looked at Dushyanta and said, "Greetings, my husband, this is our son." Dushyanta again became enraged. "Why would I, a king, father a child by you, a poor hermit woman, when I have the pick of the fairest women in my kingdom, from the richest families and the best political connections? You must be mad!"

But Shakuntala fixed a piercing gaze at Dushyanta and then told the story of how she and the king had been married.

Dushyanta knew that the old Brahman was dead, and said, "Do you have any witness to corroborate this ridiculous story?" Shakuntala then replied that there had indeed been one witness, a Brahman, who, unfortunately, was now deceased. At this, Dushyanta let out a haughty, scornful laugh. "You make this claim without a single witness and then tell me that this urchin is the heir to the throne! Get out of here while I still have a sense of humor!"

Calmly, her eyes fixed on the king, Shakuntala said, "My lord, there *were* other witnesses: Brahma, the Great Self, heard your vows. The sun, the moon, the heavens, the earth, the wind, the waters, fire, the forest creatures, and the birds of the air all heard your vows. I now call upon them all to help me."

Dushyanta again scorned her, sarcastically saying, "Woman, get out of here before you make an even greater fool of yourself!" This made the third time that Dushyanta had denied knowing Shakuntala, and by custom, the third time a lie is told, the gods take notice.

At this a voice came out of heaven and spoke, saying, "She speaks the truth, Dushyanta. Respect your wife and embrace your son and heir or die!" At this, Dushyanta solemnly climbed down from his throne and took the little boy in his arms. With tears in his eyes, he turned to Shakuntala and apologized, saying that he had acted unfairly because his courtiers would never accept a queen from such a humble estate. He begged her forgiveness, and again became so struck by her beauty after even all the intervening years, that he became a model husband. As for the boy, he was no longer called All-Tamer, but Bharata, meaning *Heaven has spoken.*

Bharata fulfilled Kanva's prophecy and was such a great emperor that his land extended from the deserts of the northwest to the snows of the Himalayas in the east and to the steamy lands of the south. The greatness of his rule made the people call the land Bharatvarsha, the land of Bharat—India.

Connections

This one episode of the vast Hindu founding epic is critical in that it is the story of how India got her name and how the qualities of King Bharata are perceived to be alive in the nation.

Shakuntala, the mother of Bharata, is that rare character in mythology: a heroine who bears the signs of the myth of the hero. She is, of course, the offspring of a mortal and a god, but as she is a *heroine*, the roles are reversed: it is her mother who is divine and her father who is mortal, in contrast to the usual elements of the hero myths. Like the heroes we have seen, Shakuntala is raised by a foster father. But where the heroic elements of Shakuntala's life leave off, they begin to manifest themselves in her son, Bharata, who shows the prodigy characteristic of all infant and child heroes across cultures. And, of course, Bharata has both royal and divine blood. There is the common heroic quest, as well, to be found in Bharata's (and what is more important, his mother's) quest to be recognized as heir to the throne. It is a struggle, and a painful wait, before Bharata's destiny can be realized.

But there is a particularly Indian element in the union of the divine *apsaras* Menaka and a holy *rishi*, something rarely seen in other cultures. The sense of Indian nationality is inextricably bound to Hindu identity, and here the legitimacy of Bharata is based as much upon descent from a holy ascetic, that most Indian of characters, as upon divine and royal ancestry. Also, it is the voice of God that gives Bharata and the nation a name. India exists because "God has spoken."

HIAWATHA TARENYAWAGON
(Iroquois)

The actual Iroquois myth of Hiawatha bears no relation to the stories contained in Henry Wadsworth Longfellow's familiar *Song of Hiawatha*. Longfellow's work portrayed Hiawatha as a hero of the Algonquins of the Lake Superior region, while the Iroquois homeland of Hiawatha was in central and western New York State and southern Ontario. The myths retold by Longfellow actually were stories of the Algonquin deity Michabo.

The myth of Hiawatha is a wonderful example of the foundation myth, documenting the founding of a nation, or in this case, the Five Nations of the Iroquois Confederacy, whose system of government served as a model to the American founding fathers in drafting the U.S. Constitution.

Tarenyawagon, the upholder of the heavens, was awakened from his slumber by horrible cries of anguish from earth. The humans were murdering each other, fighting against terrible giants, and falling into anarchy and deep despair. Taking the form of a mortal man, Tarenyawagon came to the earth, took a little girl by the hand, and led a miserable band of human refugees to a cave where he told them to sleep, for hope had now returned to humanity.

When the people had rested, Tarenyawagon again took a little girl by the hand and led the people toward the rising sun, where they built a great lodge house. There they lived happily, prospered, and had many children. As the people were now numerous, Tarenyawagon called them together and told them to form five great nations and scatter themselves throughout the land from the great river (the Hudson) to the freshwater seas (the Great Lakes). A few families first separated from the group, and Tarenyawagon named them the Tehwroga, or people of different speech. From the moment that Tarenyawagon pronounced their name, they began to speak a different language, and became the Mohawk nation. To them, Tarenyawagon gave tobacco, squash, corn, and beans, as well as dogs to help them hunt. He taught them to be great farmers and hunters. Then Tarenyawagon left, taking a little girl by the hand.

Again, Tarenyawagon separated some of the remaining families and took them to a beautiful valley. He named this group the Nehwretago, or tall tree people, in honor of the fine forests in their new homeland. They, too, had their own language, and became the Oneida nation.

Then, again taking a little girl by the hand, he led some families to a mountain called Onondaga, which was the name of this new nation. They, too, began to speak their own language.

He separated more families, and taking yet another little girl by the hand, he took them to the lake called Goyoga, and these became the Cayuga nation.

There were now but a few families left, so Tarenyawagon again took a little girl by the hand and led the families to another mountain called Canandaigua. This was the home of the people he named Tehonenoyent, the Seneca nation. Their name means *keepers of the door*, and they are the sentinels of the Five Nations.

Some of the people left the land of the Five Nations and went far to the west to another great river, called the Mississippi, but were never heard from again. The Five Nations who remained in their homeland prospered under the direction of the Mothers—the little girls who had walked with Tarenyawagon, and their daughters.

Connections

Tarenyawagon is the upholder of the heavens, and thus, there is a divine imprint on the legitimacy not only of the Five Nations Confederation, but on the founding of each of its constituent peoples.

The most significant element of this myth, however, is that Tarenyawagon takes a little girl by the hand as he founds each of the five nations. This is important, as the Iroquois were a matriarchal society, and the legitimacy of the Mothers is established by whose hands Tarenyawagon chose to hold.

THE FOUNDING OF ATHENS
(Greece)

As foundation myths are all about the collective identity of a nation or people, they often provide an insight into the character of a people. Not only does this foundation myth provide divine authority for the legitimacy of the Athenian state, it tells us what the Athenians liked best about themselves.

Zeus often enjoyed leaving Mount Olympus and strolling around the earth. On one such trip, he found the ideal location for a great city, with a natural harbor that was accessible by land from all parts of Greece. He was so delighted that he convened an assembly of the gods to inform them of his discovery. The gods listened with mounting excitement, and

soon a competition ensued as to which god would be the
patron of the new city. Two gods in particular, Poseidon, the
sea god, and Athena, the goddess of wisdom, were eager to
have the city named for them.

This placed Zeus in a difficult position, for Athena was his
beloved daughter and Poseidon, his brother. So Zeus allowed
both to make their respective cases and have the assembled
gods decide.

Poseidon pointed out that, as the city had such a wonderful
natural harbor and its inhabitants would probably be seafaring
folk, it was only natural that he should be the patron. He
would be able to summon the winds to assist trading ships,
enabling commerce to flourish. He would order the fish to
school together near the harbor to supply the city's inhabitants with food. To protect the city, he would make the
people invincible by land as well. Soon, it would be the
greatest city in the world.

Athena then argued that commercial success was all well
and good, but the trading of ideas would be as beneficial to
humankind as the trading of commodities. The world would
come to know her city as the home of art, philosophy, and literature. Such a reputation, she added, would hardly impede
commercial success.

Poseidon responded that even if the city were to be
renowned for its wisdom and culture, it would have to support
itself economically.

Athena then reminded the assembled gods that there were
already a number of prosperous seaports in the world. This
special site, chosen by Zeus himself, should be a special city,
different from any other in the world. She, as patroness,
would guarantee its economic success if she were allowed to
make this city the center of ideas.

The presentations by the two deities came perilously close to degenerating into a quarrel, so Zeus then spoke from his throne, saying, "I will give the city to the god who can bring forth from the earth some gift that is the greater blessing to the mortals who will dwell there." Then he adjourned the assembly for a short while.

Poseidon, knowing of the great wealth of the oceans, relaxed, confident of victory. Athena wanted to do all she could to be the patroness of the city, so she spoke to Demeter, the goddess of grain, and Bacchus, the god of wine. As gods of the land, they were in favor of Athena becoming the city's patroness. Demeter gave Athena the pledge that she would bless the grain that grew near the city. Bacchus promised to bless the vines. Confidently, Athena returned to the reconvened assembly.

Zeus then asked Poseidon to produce the gift he would offer to the city. Poseidon waved his hand as a huge chasm opened at his feet. Out sprang a huge white warhorse, wearing battle armor. Poseidon then told the gods that the city would be invincible in battle, with this warhorse as his gift. Poseidon then said, "I would like the city to be called Poseidonia."

All eyes then turned to Athena, who gently tapped the earth. Suddenly a green shoot popped out of the ground and grew higher and higher until it became a tree. Soon small green fruit appeared on the tree. Athena then spoke. "My gift to the people is this tree, the olive tree, to ensure the prosperity of the people of my city. I also offer my pledge of freedom and happiness for the mortals that dwell there. With my gift of wisdom, the people of my city will be able to govern themselves. Poseidon's gift is impressive, but it will bring only war and suffering to the people. My gifts will make the city the envy of the world."

The assembled gods roared their approval of Athena's gifts, and Zeus announced, "The city will be called Athens."

Connections

This foundation myth has the usual divine roots of legitimacy, but also tells us what Athenians thought of themselves, and even the basis of the Athenian economy. Unlike its rival, Sparta, or the trade cities of the Mediterranean, Athens is a city of ideas, not war. Commerce may thrive, but it is wisdom and the arts that are the distinguishing features of Athens. The blessings of wine, grain, and Athena's holy olive tree (which appeared with Athena on Greek coins in both ancient and modern times) still form the diet of Athenians today.

ROMULUS AND REMUS
(Early Rome)

The myth of Romulus and Remus clearly predates that of Aeneas, and was the founding myth of early Rome. The story tells of a very different Rome than in the Imperial period—a simpler, more agrarian society that gave birth to the Roman Republic.

Romulus and Remus were the twin sons of the war god Mars and the vestal (former) virgin, Rhea Silvia. Of course, their birth, were it known, would have caused the virgin to lose not only her post as vestal virgin, but her life as well. The twins were placed in a basket and put on the Tiber River, where the basket floated until it beached at the grotto of Lupercal. A she-wolf took the boys as her own and suckled them until a kind shepherd named Faustulus and his wife, Acca, adopted them.

When the brothers had grown to manhood, they decided to found a city on the Tiber. In choosing the site, they were careful to consult the omens and particularly watched the birds. Near the site of present-day Rome, they encountered an augur (soothsayer), who pointed to the sky with his staff. In the section of the sky apportioned to Romulus, there were twelve vultures. In that apportioned to Remus, there were only six.

Romulus proceeded to divide the new city with two parts for himself and one for his brother. As Romulus plowed a furrow to mark the boundaries, Remus began mocking him and complaining about the unjust division of the land. Having had enough, Romulus slew his brother. All the ruling families of Rome claim descent from him.

Connections

In the story of Romulus and Remus, we see some very familiar heroic images: they are the twin sons of the god Mars and Rhea Silvia but, in this instance, raised by a she-wolf as foster mother and then by a kindly shepherd. The myth has a great deal to say about how early Romans saw themselves: they had inherited the warlike character of Mars, softened by the woodland character of the vestal virgin Silvia, whose name means *of the forest*. As in the Tangun myth from Korea, an animal's character is taken by the founder and his descendants. Romulus and Remus "took" the character of the she-wolf with her milk. The wolf is admired for its courage, cunning, and ferocity, and these are qualities that Romans saw in themselves.

There are two interesting parallels with the Bible stories familiar to us: the casting of the infant twins on the Tiber in a basket recalls Moses, and the killing of Remus reminds us of the story of Cain and Abel.

Some commentators have been troubled by Romulus's murder of his twin. The partition of Rome appears to be unfair, with twice the land apportioned to Romulus as is apportioned to Remus. But to the Romans, the story was an object lesson in accepting the portion given one by the gods without questioning. As early Rome was a society that depended heavily on slave labor, this, too, tells us about the character of the Roman state.

AENEAS
(Imperial Rome [and then Britain])

Ancient Rome had a problem as it went from republic to empire: it lacked its own heroic founding epic and cultural hero. And as heir to the Greek civilization, it was imperative that the foundation myth have roots in the Greek epic, the *Iliad*. Also, as the emperor Augustus was a god, the emperor needed a divine genealogy; the Roman poet Virgil (70–19 B.C.) responded to this with Rome's own epic, the *Aeneid*. The hero was Aeneas, a son of the goddess Venus. Aeneas had played a rather small role in the Homeric epic, and fled Troy with no further information supplied by Homer. Virgil had Aeneas landing in Italy. But, there was a problem: the Trojan War predated the founding of Rome by some four hundred to five hundred years. So, Virgil made sure that Aeneas stopped at the site of Rome and prophesied about its greatness.

The names of the gods are, of course, the Roman names: Venus (Greek: Aphrodite), Juno (Greek: Hera), and Jupiter (Greek: Zeus).

Aeneas was the son of the Trojan noble Anchises and the goddess Venus. He was also the son-in-law of King Priam of Troy. After the Greeks had gained entrance inside the walls of Ilium (Troy) through the Trojan horse, they burned the city to the ground. Among the dead was Aeneas's wife. Aeneas fled the ruined city, carrying his aging father, Anchises, on his back. (Anchises had been struck lame for having the audacity as a mortal to sleep with Venus.)

Aeneas led his sons, Anchises, and a party of Trojan nobles from Troy to first arrive in Thrace, on the Greek mainland, where Aeneas attempted to found a new city. As he prepared to offer the requisite burnt sacrifices to the gods, he gathered together some wood. As Aeneas broke off a branch from one bush, a voice cried out, begging him to spare it. It so happened that this bush was the remains of the Trojan prince, Polydorus (many gifts), who had been sent by King Priam to Thrace for safety during the war. Polydorus had come bearing treasures for the rulers of Thrace, to be exchanged for asylum. But the treacherous Thraceans set upon him, stole the treasures, shot his body full of arrows, and now the body had turned into this bush. Upon hearing the story of the evil people of Thrace, Aeneas immediately led the Trojans onward.

Their next stop was the island of Delos, where the god Apollo and his sister, the hunting goddess, Diana (Greek: Artemis), had been born. This was the site of Apollo's oracle, whom Aeneas consulted for advice on his journey. The oracle advised Aeneas to "seek his mother in a land where the race of

Aeneas will dwell, prosper, and rule over many nations, including the Greeks." This didn't make sense to Aeneas, so he asked his father for an interpretation. Anchises told Aeneas that a family tradition held that Aeneas's ancestors had originally come from the west, from Italy. Italy alone could be the ordained destination of the Trojan refugees. As to "following his mother," this meant that Venus would be with them throughout the journey.

The oracle's prophecy was confirmed by a dream, in which the gods called Aeneas to go to the land where his ancestor Dardanus had lived. Dardanus was said to have come from Italy, in the area of Latium.

The Trojans continued to stop at many islands and have many adventures, but the rigors of the journey proved too great for old Anchises, who died happy in knowing that his son would be the founder of a great city.

One of Aeneas's stops was Carthage, which was founded by colonists from Tyre (in present-day Lebanon) and now ruled by Queen Dido. Dido herself was the daughter of the king of Tyre, and she assumed rule of the city after the death of her husband.

Juno had never forgiven the Trojans since the Trojan Paris had judged a beauty contest and bypassed her for Venus, Aeneas's mother. Out of spite, she wanted Aeneas to fall in love with Dido and abandon his plans to found a great city. So Venus allowed Aeneas to fall in love with Dido, as she felt sorry for her widowed son. The two fell hopelessly in love, and life with Dido in Carthage was so pleasant that soon Aeneas hardly gave a thought to Italy.

Jupiter finally sent Mercury (Greek: Hermes), the shrewd messenger of the gods, to remind Aeneas of his mission. Aeneas was so in love with Dido that he tried to argue with

Mercury, but no mortal can resist that god's keen words and it was clear to Aeneas that he had to press onward to Italy. Aeneas told Dido that he had to continue onward to fulfill his destiny. At first Dido merely pleaded with him to stay with her in her kingdom. Then she got angry. As the Trojan ships were leaving Carthage, Dido prepared a huge funeral pyre and flung herself upon it to her death. The people of Carthage never forgave Aeneas or his descendants for Dido's death, until Rome ultimately destroyed the city centuries later.

Aeneas's ship finally landed on the banks of the Tiber River, where Rome lies today. The surrounding land of Latium was ruled by the elderly King Latinus, who had only one child, Lavinia. Lavinia was beautiful, and many noble families sent their sons to her as suitors, including King Turnus of the Rutulians. Without male issue, Latinus's kingdom would pass to another royal house, so Latinus was eager to see his daughter marry. However, Lavinia rejected all her suitors, including Turnus, and so Latinus reminded his daughter that an oracle had predicted that her husband would come from a far-off land and that together they would create a royal house that would rule the world.

Aeneas sent a legation of one hundred Trojans to Latinus, who immediately recognized Aeneas as the promised husband of Lavinia. But, upon arrival at the site of Rome, Aeneas had consulted an oracle, the sibyl, who informed Aeneas that he could not win in battle, marry Lavinia, or claim the right to rule Italy without first passing through the underworld. The sibyl knew that Aeneas missed his father, Anchises, and wanted to see him before his marriage. The sibyl also knew that Aeneas grieved deeply over his fallen Trojan comrades and thoughts of them impeded Aeneas from concentrating entirely on his quest.

Yet the path to the underworld was a gloomy one, shrouded in darkness. The sibyl suggested that Aeneas sacrifice four black bulls to Hecate, goddess of the night, to earn her assistance. As the smoke from the sacrifice drifted high, thunder sounded and the earth quaked. The sibyl then pointed to a tree with a golden bough, advising Aeneas to break off the bough before journeying further.

Aeneas and the sibyl then entered the mouth of the underworld, walking past the horrible spirits of Discord, Disease, Hunger, and War, all of whom periodically walked the earth claiming mortals for this dark kingdom. They then passed a field occupied by the hapless souls who had not been properly buried and were destined to wander for one hundred years before gaining admittance into the underworld. Next they came to the banks of the River Styx, where Charon, the ferryman, gruffly informed them that the dead, and not the living, were his passengers; therefore, he would not take them across. However, Aeneas showed Charon the golden bough, and the ferryman then conducted them across the Styx.

The boat passed by the field of mourning, where tragic young lovers who had committed suicide wandered together as couples. They also passed the seats of the three judges of the dead.

Then they came to a fork in the river. From the left they heard the terrible screams of the punished souls. To the right they saw the purple rays of light emanating from the Elysian fields where the good and great dwelled in everlasting bliss. The sibyl then instructed Aeneas to place the golden bough in the rock wall opposite the fork in the river. After he did so, Charon veered sharply to the right, toward the Elysian fields. There Aeneas saw great poets, sages, heroes, and others. The

Trojan hero Ajax, Aeneas's old comrade, was there and remained silent. Also among the dead was Dido, who refused to acknowledge Aeneas. Soon Aeneas saw his father, Anchises. When the ferry landed, father and son embraced. Anchises said that his son would be the founder of the greatest empire ever known. As they parted, Anchises took Aeneas to the well of Lethe (forgetfulness), from which all mortals must drink before leaving the underworld. The sibyl then conducted Aeneas safely to the land above the ground, where he would at last realize his destiny.

Things were so pleasant in Italy that Juno again decided to send Discord to stir up strife by building opposition toward Aeneas and Latinus among the other Italian tribes. So one day when Aeneas's son Iulus was hunting, Discord caused his hounds to smell the scent of a pet deer that belonged to King Turnus's daughter, Silvia. Iulus killed the deer with his javelin, and it fell dead at the princess's feet. Turnus took this as a deliberate provocation and vowed to make war on Latinus, the Trojans, and their allies—for Turnus had never gotten over Lavinia's rejection of him as suitor.

Father Tiber, spirit of the river, appeared to Aeneas in a dream and affirmed that Italy was truly the hero's home and destiny. Proud that Aeneas and his descendants would build the center of a great empire on his shores, the river god informed Aeneas that Evander, a Greek who now ruled an Italian tribe, the Arcadians, had long desired to defeat Turnus. Tiber implored Aeneas to find Evander and form an alliance. More importantly, Aeneas was told that it was time to appease Juno before she came to the aid of Turnus. Upon awakening from the dream, Aeneas immediately made a sacrifice to Juno and then set off in search of Evander. He found

Evander speaking to his son. Both pledged their support to Aeneas, which was all the more meaningful as Evander was the son of Greek heroes, Aeneas's erstwhile enemies.

Jupiter had grown tired of his wife Juno's harassment of Aeneas and persuaded her to stop. Aeneas's sacrifice had also helped to soften her wrath. Moreover, as the patroness of marriage, Juno knew that she would be bound to support the marriage of Aeneas and Lavinia. With Juno thus appeased, Aeneas was assured of victory.

With the assistance of his allies, Aeneas went to meet Turnus in battle. Among the assembled enemies was the tyrant Mezentius, who had exacted tribute from all the tribes of Italy, including the Latins. Mezentius had a son named Lausus, who was as brave a warrior as had ever stood in the field.

When Mezentius met Aeneas on the battlefield, he immediately threw his spear at Aeneas. It deflected off Aeneas's shield. Lausus then ran to place himself between his father and Aeneas's spear. Just as other warriors began to whisk Mezentius off to safety, Aeneas's spear struck brave Lausus. Aeneas was so moved by Lausus's bravery and filial piety that he delayed in striking a fatal blow until he could assure Lausus of a funeral worthy of his bravery and honor. With the death of Lausus, Mezentius lost all fear and flung himself at Aeneas's sword, thereby meeting his own death.

The stage was thus set for the final encounter between Turnus and Aeneas. First Turnus encountered Evander's son, Pallas, who conducted himself so bravely that even harsh Turnus wept as Pallas fell. The usual custom was to strip the bodies of one's enemies and seize their arms and treasure as booty. Pallas wore a golden belt and had the finest arms in the land, yet Turnus so respected him that he left the belt and arms in place for the young hero's own comrades to keep.

Juno, once the patroness of Turnus, had not informed him that she had withdrawn her support. So, Turnus threw himself at Aeneas with the confidence of one certain of divine support. But Venus had rendered her son's armor invulnerable, and so Turnus's blows were harmless. Turnus now knew that his time had come and pleaded for his life, like a weakling. Aeneas could see the golden belt glistening on the corpse of Pallas, and thinking of his brave young comrade versus the cowardly Turnus, Aeneas dealt Turnus the fatal blow, crying, "Pallas deals you this blow."

Aeneas then married Lavinia and founded the town of Lavinium near Rome. Aeneas's son, Iulus, was the ancestor of the clan Julii, which produced Julius Caesar and the Julian dynasty of emperors. Iulus himself founded the town of Alba Longa, where Romulus and Remus were later born.

Connections

This is both a classic hero myth and a founding myth, with all of the elements of both. The Julian emperors, including the divine Augustus, could now claim legitimacy based upon a genealogy tracing back to the goddess Venus. And now there was a mythic basis for the long-standing enmity between Rome and Carthage.

The necessary element of tying the divine origin of the rulers to the soil is tenuous at best in Aeneas, as he came from elsewhere. Each of the regions that posed a threat to Aeneas also were particularly troublesome to Rome. Moreover, Rome had a history of little wars with various tribes of Italy that is reflected in the myth of Aeneas.

The Aeneas story as a foundation myth was the heroic antidote to the Romans' slight inferiority complex with respect to

Greece. While the Romans had established a vast empire and taken on much of Greek culture, Greek intellectual achievement still dominated much of the eastern half of the empire and was cited as the authoritative source in the west, as well. In the Aeneas story, Virgil provided a basis for the conquest of Greece and a source of revenge, both for the Trojans and for the Romans, who were, despite being conquerors, still considered barbarians when compared to the peoples of Athens.

BRUTUS
(Britain)

The British, emerging as an empire and searching for linkages to classical antiquity to bolster the legitimacy of the imperial mission, looked to Rome and offered an addendum to the story of Aeneas that provided the appropriate genealogy for their nation.

> For noble Britons sprung from Trojan bold
> and Troynovant was built of old Troy's ashes cold.

—Sir Edmund Spenser, *The Faerie Queen*, Book III, Canto IX

Brutus was the son of Silvius, the grandson of Aeneas. In Italy, the descendants of Aeneas prospered and never forgot their Trojan ancestry. Brutus was hunting one day with his father and accidentally killed him. For this, Brutus was sentenced to exile. He at first fled to the Trojan colony of Epirus, in Greece, where Helenus and Andromache had once welcomed Aeneas in his travels. But the Trojans who lived there now were in great difficulty, as they were ruled by a Greek tyrant named Pandrasus. When Brutus arrived in Epirus, the news spread quickly that a Trojan champion had come to save them, and the Trojans took heart. Brutus called them all together in a forest, and the Trojans then sent a bold ultimatum to Pandrasus, informing the tyrant that they would no longer be his slaves or offer him tribute. As Trojans, it was beneath them to be subject to anyone but another Trojan. Pandrasus was unprepared for such a bold statement, and knowing of Aeneas's prowess, he capitulated. Brutus then married Pandrasus's daughter, Imogen, and explained that he, like Aeneas, had a divine destiny to realize. Pandrasus saw the will of the gods in this, so he outfitted Brutus and the Trojans with a fleet of 320 ships.

On the third day at sea, the Trojans found themselves on an island, uninhabited but covered with artifacts of its former inhabitants, who had been of a noble race. Brutus found a temple of Diana (Greek: Artemis) in ruins and began to offer sacrifices. Weary, he fell asleep there. The goddess then appeared to him and announced that he, too, would be the founder of a great race that would rule many nations. The land was far to the west, beyond Gaul, and known as Albion, the former abode of a race of giants. Brutus gathered his fleet and immediately sailed for Gaul, where some of his cousins from Italy joined him.

They landed in what is now Devonshire and traveled until they came to a river that reminded them of the Tiber—the Thames. Brutus and his company built a city there and called it Troyanova (New Troy), which in time became London.

After a twenty-four-year reign, Brutus died and the kingdom was divided among his three sons. The north was ruled by Albanach, founder of Scotland (*Alba* is Gaelic for *Scotland*). The west was ruled by another son, Camber (Wales is known as Cambria, or Cymru in Welsh). The rest of the land, which we now call England, was ruled by Brutus's son Locrine, who had married Gwendolyn, the daughter of Corineus (whence comes Cornwall), a Gaulish king.

The descendants of Brutus called the island Brutannia or Brytannia in his honor, and King Arthur is said to be Brutus's direct descendant.

Connections

The most important element of British national identity contained in this myth is the integration of Scotland, Wales, Cornwall, and England into one Great Britain. The three sons of Brutus are Albanach (Scotland), Camber (Wales), and Locrine, which some have tied to the name Lancaster, as in the once-royal House of Lancaster's English kings. Cornwall is represented in Locrine's wife.

The integration of two other nations, Scotland and Wales, each with its own proud history, tradition, culture, and language, into a Great Britain under an essentially English monarch requires an appropriate civic myth that points all three to a common origin. Lest you doubt, however, that this myth came from England, remember that the New Troy is built at London—not Cardiff or Edinburgh.

This integrated Great Britain, destined to be a great empire, is built by the descendants of the heroes of classical antiquity. This speaks to the British self-perception as guardians of civilization and high culture. Indeed, during the British "Augustan" age of the kings of the House of Hanover and even into Victorian times, British empire-builders spoke of themselves as the rightful heirs of empire, worthy of Roman heritage, who in turn claimed Aeneas as founder.

THE FOUNDING OF IRAN
(Ancient Persia)

The state religion of pre-Islamic Iran was Zoroastrianism, which is predicated on the belief that the entire cosmos is consumed by the struggle between Ormazd, the good lord of light, and Ahriman, the evil lord of darkness. The Persian shahs believed that they were Ormazd's surrogates in the earthly episodes of this struggle, even as their enemies were surrogates of Ahriman. The legitimacy of the Persian shahs rested on their descent from the great hero–kings and the belief that they were "Ormazd's hands" on the earth.

The entire cosmos is the battleground for the Great Duality. Ormazd, the lord of light and source of all good, is in constant battle with Ahriman, the evil one. In the earliest times, Ormazd had subdued Ahriman and chained the evil one to a rock in hell for a thousand years. During this period, humankind enjoyed a millennium of prosperity, peace, long life, and freedom from disease under the great shah Jamshid. With the rule of righteousness, Jamshid was free to invent iron, the plow, weapons, the cultivation of silk, the making of perfumes and medicines, and establish the arts. Jamshid knew that the day would come when Ahriman was freed from his sentence, and when the thousand years had come to an end, Jamshid feared the worst. But nothing happened. For evil is subtle and Ahriman waited until Jamshid had been lulled into false security.

In a neighboring kingdom was a prince named Zohak. Ahriman took on human guise and went to Zohak's palace to apply for the job of chief cook, and was promptly hired. Day after day, Ahriman prepared delicious, sumptuous feasts for

Zohak; with each meal Zohak ate, the more evil he became. One day Zohak summoned his chef to compliment him, and asked, "Is there any reward in my kingdom I can offer you in thanks for your fine cuisine?" The cunning Ahriman, feigning humility, replied, "I only wish to embrace you, my lord, and kiss your shoulders as a sign of my loyalty!" Zohak agreed, and no sooner had Ahriman embraced the king than the possession of Zohak became complete. Two vile black poisonous vipers sprang from Zohak's shoulders and demanded to be fed the still-warm brains of human beings from now on. Now Ahriman was ready to take the throne from Jamshid.

Jamshid was so used to peace and so complacent that he had forgotten to post guards at his palace or even maintain an army. So Zohak easily subdued Jamshid, sawed his body in half, and took Jamshid's two daughters prisoner. With this began a thousand years of the rule of darkness, a time when evil permeated everything on earth. This was a time of murder, misery, chaos, and every manner of horror. Life never ended naturally, as rape and murder prevailed. Naked, starving orphans roamed the land, as their murdered parents would never be able to know old age. Ormazd witnessed this with great grief and decided to send a champion to save the people.

One night Zohak found himself tormented by a dream in which he saw himself in chains, bowing before a conquering young prince. The troubled king called a sage to interpret the dream. The sage bluntly told Zohak that his thousand years were up and the new prince, who would be named Feridun, would easily subdue the evil king. With that, Zohak ordered the murder of every little boy in the kingdom.

A virtuous woman of noble birth named Firanak gave birth to a baby boy and named him Feridun, hid him in a garden, and later had a kindly shepherd take the boy to safety in India.

As he grew up, Feridun heard of the horrors and cruelties that Zohak had visited upon his homeland, and the young prince vowed to free his people.

Zohak was seized by such paranoia about his overthrow that he was unable to sleep and grew frail. One day when Zohak was in his palace, a brave smith named Kavé appeared and denounced the evil ruler. Kavé's two sons had been murdered so that their brains could be fed to the serpents. Kavé had also had a dream of the champion and told Zohak that he, Kavé, would summon the one who would free the nation. Kavé then put his smith's apron on a pole as a battle banner and left the palace unharmed, as Zohak was so stunned by this challenge that he could not move.

Kavé gathered a band of men and set out for India, where the dream had told him the champion would be found. Guided by angels, the ever growing army found Feridun, who knew that this was his call to battle.

Feridun met little resistance as he approached the palace of Zohak, where he freed Jamshid's daughters, whom he married. Zohak was out when Feridun arrived, and soon the evil king appeared at the gates, brandishing a sword. But so impressive was Feridun's bravery that the now frail Zohak had difficulty striking. Just as Feridun was about to deliver the fatal blow of his battle club to Zohak, an angel appeared and ordered Feridun not to kill Zohak, but to chain him to a rock. And so, Zohak bowed before Feridun in chains, as the dream had ordained.

Feridun reigned over the land for five hundred years. Purged of evil, the people enjoyed a prosperity and peace unknown since the time of Jamshid. As Feridun grew old, he decided to divide the kingdom among his three sons.

The most virtuous of the sons was Irej, or Irah, to whom

Feridun gave the land that would someday be known by Irej's name as Iran. To Salm, the ancestor of the Greeks and Europeans, Feridun gave the west. To Tur was given the east, China and Turkestan. (Note: The ancient Persians called the Mongols and Turks Turanians.) Salm and Tur, however, were angry that Irej had the best realm, so they promptly made war. Irej went to meet his brothers on the field of battle.

Irej attempted to make peace with his brothers by offering all manner of concessions, but Tur first smashed Irej's skull and then stabbed his brothers with a dagger.

Feridun had been anxiously awaiting Irej's return, and the old king's heart raced when he saw the armies returning under the smith's apron banner. When Feridun went to greet his son, one of Kavé's descendants told him the sad news and presented Irej's skull, which Tur had stuffed with perfume, as a grisly message from his evil son. Enraged, Feridun prayed to Ormazd for a champion. The champion was Manucher, Feridun's great-grandson, the grandson of Irej. The brave lad easily defeated his cruel granduncles, named the land Iran in honor of Irej, and took the crown of all three lands upon the death of Feridun. Still, enough of the descendants of Salm and Tur remained to torment the Iranians, but the shahs have the blood of Jamshid, Feridun, and Manucher in their veins and can still subdue the foreigners. Thus, the shahs are the force for human good on this earth, and one of their titles is "Ormazd's hands on the earth."

Connections

The eternal contest between Ormazd and Ahriman plays itself out in the lives of men and nations. The noble *(arya)* nation of Iran is the temporal force of good in the world, and its shah is responsible for the preservation of all that is goodness and righteousness, not merely in his realm, but in the world.

The foundation myth of ancient Persia also offers up the elements of how the nation got its name, Iran, the line of legitimate kingship, and an explanation for the everlasting enmity between the Iranians and Turanians—one that is reminiscent of the hatred between Rome and Carthage. The legitimacy of the shah in this instance is not based on divine ancestry, but on the mythical establishment of the shah as Ormazd's surrogate.

The myth of Feridun has some interesting parallels with the other myths of the hero, such as Theseus, Cuchulain, and others. There is once more the familiar theme of the threat against the life of the young hero, the flight to safety, and the protection of guardians. It is to be remembered that ancient Persia was an integral part of the northern Eurasian myth-producing area that included the Greeks, Celts, Norse, and Indians. The Persian language is related to the languages of these peoples.

The sense of the self-perception of the Iranian people—as the force of good in the world battle against evil—has survived the collapse of the ancient Persian empire and the introduction of Islam, and is an element still recognizable in the ideology of the present Islamic republic of Iran. The depiction of the United States as "the Great Satan" by Iran's present rulers is more easily understood in that their ancient Persian ancestors perceived themselves as "Ormazd's hands on earth," battling against their enemies, whom they personified as agents of the evil one, Ahriman.

The Persian past has not been entirely subsumed by Shiite Islam. Jamshid, Feridun, and Manucher are all relatively

common names for Iranian men today. While Shiites
presently deplore the religion of their ancestors and persecute
the few remaining Zoroastrians, the tale of Feridun is still
sung today and even presented in folk dramas throughout
Iran. The retelling is a reminder of the ancient belief that Iran
has a special mission of good in an evil world.

THE FOUNDING OF THE EMPIRE
(Japan)

Amaterasu, the sun goddess, was an ancestor of the emperor.
She watched from her Celestial Deity Palace while Okuninushi, the hero, wisely ruled Japan. While she was favorably
impressed by her nephew, it irked her that her islands were
ruled by the family of her obnoxious brother, Susanowo, the
wind god. In addition, she thought that the compassionate
Okuninushi was too soft. He had not subdued a number of
very nasty earth-devils who were causing all manner of problems. So she decreed that her son, Oshihomimi, should rule
on the earth, and she sent several expeditions to unseat Okuninushi. Her forces defeated those of Okuninushi, who then
agreed to abdicate on the condition that he would be considered a god, not merely a hero, and be worshiped at his temple
in Izumo (where he is now worshiped both as the Shinto *kami*
Okuninushi and the very popular Buddhist deity, Daikoku, or
great land).

Amaterasu commanded Oshihomimi to rule the land, but
Oshihomimi suggested that his little son Ninigi rule instead.
She agreed, and sent her grandson to earth with sacred rice to
grow and offer in sacrifice to the Celestial Deities. She gave
him the mirror that had been used in coaxing her from her

cave, which people would henceforth worship, considering it to be a reflection of Amaterasu's own spirit. She also gave him a sword and a curved jewel and the three sacred jewels that became the symbols of the emperor's legitimacy, and remain so to this day.

On earth, Ninigi was faced with a tough decision: There were two daughters of the *kami* of Mount Takachiho on the island of Kyūshū, and the mountain deity offered Ninigi his choice of the daughters. The first daughter was Princess Iwanaga (Eternal Rock), who was ugly but could convey the power of longevity, even immortality, through sex. The second daughter was the Princess Konohanasakuya (Flower Blossoms), who was absolutely beautiful, but vapid.

Ninigi chose Konohanasakuya, who conceived a baby immediately after sleeping with him. Ninigi could not believe that his wife could become pregnant so quickly and suspected that she had been unfaithful. Konohanasakuya offered to demonstrate her faithfulness by entering a palace without doors, then setting fire to the palace just as she went into labor. Not only did she do this and survive, she had triplets! This not only proved her innocence but made her the valuable bearer of royal heirs.

Two of these children were Umisachi-Hiko, a great fisherman, and his brother, the hunter Yamasachi-Hiko. They once decided to trade professions for a day, but Yamasachi dropped his brother's fishhook into the sea and caught nothing. Umisachi then explained that one should always stick to one's own assigned job, as the power to conduct that job never passes with the tools alone. Thus, having a fishhook does not make a hunter into a fisherman. Yamasachi broke his sword into many tiny fishhooks to offer as compensation to his brother, but Umisachi did not accept them. Instead, Umisachi demanded that his brother find the original fishhook, from wherever it was in the sea.

Yamasachi decided to ask the help of the sea god. He then fell in love with the sea god's daughter, Princess Toyotama, and slept with her. The sea god was impressed by Yamasachi and readily accepted him as a son-in-law. Yamasachi remained with them for three years, at which point the sea god called upon the fish to find the hook. One of the fish, who had swallowed the hook, spat it up. Yamasachi returned the hook to his brother, but Umisachi still would not forgive him. Using a magic jewel, Yamasachi then caused his brother to suffer great pain until Umisachi agreed to serve him as sentry.

Princess Toyotama, who was about to have a baby, warned her husband, Yamasachi, that she would not be able to give birth in the sea to a child of a Celestial Deity. She would have to turn into her real sea form as a crocodile, so she implored her husband to go away and not look at her. Instead, Yamasachi hid while she gave birth, and was horrified when he spied his beautiful wife turning into a grotesque, scaly giant crocodile as she bore their son. Angry that her husband had secretly watched her during labor, Princess Toyotama fled into the sea, leaving her infant son on dry land.

This boy grew up to marry the sea princess Tamayori and had four children, the eldest of whom was the first emperor, Jimmu, founder of the line that rules Japan today. And so, Japan and her emperor are the children of Heaven, Earth, and Sea.

Connections

If you are looking for a myth that has had an impact on modern history, the myth of Amaterasu is certainly one. According to the *Kojiki*, the earliest chronicle of Japan, Amaterasu was the great-great-grandmother of Jimmu, the first emperor, and a direct ancestor of the current emperor. Because of his divine ancestry, the emperor was for centuries considered to be a living god.

The mirror and curved jewel described in this myth are two of the three sacred objects that are emblems of the emperor that are guarded in the temple at Ise (the third is the sword given to Ninigi by Amaterasu). The objects supposedly remain in the temple today, although no one but the emperor and attending priests may see them. The mirror is one of the most common symbols of Shinto (Shinto is the state religion of Japan). It may be a sacred object of worship, and the mirror is valued because it is a source of honesty. It hides nothing and has a clean light that reflects everything as it is.

This myth profoundly affected modern history. A very potent belief in Japan until the 1940s was that the emperor, or *tennō*, was perceived as divine; no Japanese could ever look directly on the "August visage." Indeed, prior to World War II, Emperor Hirohito did not receive normal physical examinations, as no doctor could touch the divine emperor. Foreign observers noted that Hirohito's clothing never seemed to fit him very well; that was because no tailor was allowed to touch Hirohito's body to take measurements. In fact, it was only with great shock and dismay that the Japanese people heard the actual recorded voice of the emperor (speaking an archaic court dialect of Japanese that few could completely understand) announcing that the Pacific War had "not gone to Japan's advantage." Because the issue of divinity had not yet been settled, the broadcast was not allowed to be heard live. (Note: In 1946, the emperor formally renounced his divinity before the Japanese people.)

What kind of god, precisely, did the Japanese consider the

emperor to be? The Japanese traditionally believe in *kami*, which we recognize from the word *kamikaze* (divine wind). The *kami* encompass a wide range of spiritual beings that include the spirits of mountains, plants, tutelary deities of the home, and so forth, to the point where Japanese Christians refer to the Semitic monotheistic God as Kamisama, the Lord Kami. Because of an emperor's divine ancestry, he is viewed as a *kami*—a Superior Being.

In Aisaburo Akiyama's 1936 book, *Shinto Architecture*, he writes:

> To pay the most fervent reverence and to show a sense of the utmost devotion to the Emperor is the ultimate object of the National Faith Shinto. The Emperor of Japan is a legitimate descendant of the kami, so that he is compared to the Heaven and Earth for His righteous rule, virtue, and justice, graciously bestowing peace and happiness on the nation. That is the reason why He is revered as the Heavenly Son, just and benevolent beyond word, offering to His people an equal opportunity in all cases so as to enable them to enjoy national growth without being disturbed in the least.

The last two chapters have discussed the myths as speaking to our human identity, both individually and collectively. And in the chapters before, we have looked at myth as expressions of meaning and means to finding meaning in human experience in various contexts. We have examined the question of the parts. Now it is time to consider the whole.

Conclusion:
The Eternal Mirror

A living myth is one that speaks to the human experience across time, geography, and culture. The truth contained in these myths speaks to our own experience, individually and collectively, and helps us to participate in the legacy of all humanity. To our modern ears, however, *living myth* at first sounds like a paradox. And in the myths, truth is often contained in a paradox.

We began our inquiry by making the distinction between the causative mode of thinking—the empirical world of objective fact—and the purposive mode, which deals with values and meaning and is the realm of myth. Throughout the myths presented here, the questions of purpose and the meaning of human experience has been asked in a variety of universal human situations, with an answer that is felt as much as heard. Myth speaks to us in paradox and dilemma.

For example, with the relationship between father and son, the love of the father, Helios, is so great that he would deny his son Phaëthon the one request the boy asks, in order to save his son's life. But he cannot deny Phaëthon's request without breaking an oath binding even to the gods. Helios is bound to keep his oath—yet love requires that he break it. A similar conflict arises when Cuchulain binds his son, Connla, to the warrior's oath that requires one to battle all comers; this leads to Cuchulain's tragic slaying of his own son. And Abraham's covenant to God requires absolute obedience, to the point of Abraham's being ready to put the knife to his much-beloved son, Isaac. The purposive sense of these stories gives them their poignancy. And in them we see our own conflicts between love and duty and the paradox of human existence.

The paradox of life and death is set before us as well in the myths. In order to continue with the quest and obtain great-ness, or even immortality, the hero must go to the land of the dead. The Kore myth is an ancient causative tale of the origin of spring, as is the Norse tale of Idun—but the purposive mes-sage in both is that the descent to the world of the dead is a necessary condition of the human experience and the renewal of life.

The paradox of romantic love, as it exists with sensuality and selfishness, is seen in the myths. The butterfly and its metamorphosis is the very syntax of the purposive message of love's power to transform. Lovers, separated in life, are united in death to give us the comforting and healing message that love is stronger than death. "Nala and Damayanti" speaks both to this reality and also to the paradox that, in order to gain, one must lose.

The hero is an inherent paradox in that he is marked as a hero both by divine parentage and the tragic reality of mor-tality. Born to greatness, the hero has to become a hero; he has to be defeated before conquering, to risk annihilation in youth in order to gain immortality. The hero has recognizable human flaws that can destroy him, and faces transcendence only after the great defeat or the experience of, as in the Cuchulain myth, "weariness unto death." The paradox of the divine and the mortal is at the core of every hero and, arguably, every human life. Each of us, whether believer or nonbeliever, also either feels or yearns for a connection to a transcending truth; we refer to ourselves as "children of God" while recognizing our mortality.

Our identity as individuals finds a paradox in the collective identity of the state. The legitimacy of the state rests on the union of the sacred and the profane, on the union of divine authority with the soil. It is not by chance that American coins bear the motto "In God We Trust" or that the U.S. Capitol contains the Constantino Brumidi painting, *The Apotheosis of Washington*, where a toga-clad "Father of Our Country" is welcomed into the immortals in such a manner that an ancient Roman might easily mistake him for Aeneas. In Britain and Canada, the coins bear the image of a queen who is *Dei Gratia Regina* (By the grace of God, Queen) and bears the title of Defender of the Faith. Even secular states maintain the bonds between the sacred and profane. And there is another great paradox as well, in that the collective identity of a state is derived from the realization of the quest of an individual hero.

The sense of truth and human existence as paradoxes forms the basis of the philosophy of the contemporary French philosopher Paul Ricoeur, whose thinking has guided our inquiry into the myths (see page 3). Ricoeur's studies of myth led to a view of human beings as fallible or fragile, "suspended between a pole of infinitude and a pole of finitude." For Ricoeur, it is no surprise that the truths of human experience are conveyed as paradoxes, for the human being himself or herself is a paradox.

Ricoeur wrote that *myths are an expression of the pathos of this paradoxical human condition* of "suspension" between the infinity of the noumena and the finitude of the objective phenomena. The two poles of our existence, according to his philosophy, are the vital, aimed at the achievement of pleasure, and the spiritual, the end of which is happiness. For Ricoeur, a meaningful life is one wherein these two poles are integrated and nourish each other. The entire search for a meaningful life is to know these two opposites and create a synthesis. The human faculty that Ricoeur believed created such a necessary synthesis was our ability to feel. Myths are *documents of feeling*. The myths are the record of the human attempt to reconcile the paradox of human existence and living tools of reconciliation.

We began our inquiry by citing Ricoeur's six critical elements of the human condition: (1) our *finitude*; (2) our *estrangement* from God and/or the numinous; (3) our process of *becoming and transcendence*, in that in each human life, the truth is never whole and complete; (4) the paradox of *the freedom and burden of human choice*; (5) *our existence with, in, and through others*, for our sense of meaning is relational; and ultimately, (6) our *identity and participation* in the cosmos.

Upon our initial reading of the myths in this book, it was easy to see how individual myths expressed one of these elements as a key theme. But now it is time to consider how these elements permeate all the myths, even as they permeate our own existence.

The myths of fathers and sons, of course, speak to the identity inherent in that relationship, but there is also the poignant sense of Phaëthon, the mortal, seeking to take on the work of his divine father without the abilities conveyed by divinity.

This brings to mind the sense of finitude and estrangements from the numinous. We see ourselves faced by individual and collective tasks that are beyond the ability of a mortal human being. We see the anguish of the freedom and burden of choice inherent in Helios's and Abraham's dealings with their sons and recognize the element in our own lives. We see that a son grows into the stature of father through the failings of youth in the stories "Grandfather, Father, and Son" and "Odin and Thor." And we recognize our own process of becoming. Particularly in the case of "Grandfather, Father, and Son," we see that we, too, are social beings who live our existence in, with, and through others. Whether in our own lives, or in the myths, all of these elements of human existence interact.

The stories of romantic love are eternal tales of how humans live out their existence in, with, and through the lives of the beloved, but there is also the joyful message that love is stronger than death that speaks to our estrangement and finitude. The lovers are faced with the freedom and burden of choice; there is a cost to loving. The great tales of romantic love are the story of becoming, of an ongoing process of growth that is nurtured and fueled by love. "Nala and Damayanti," in particular, speaks to love as the catalyst of becoming, a power to transform. Our identity and participation in the cosmos is clear, as we are part of the cycle of life and death.

The myths of nature and human nature speak to our identity as beings of the earth who still perceive a divinity that makes us different from all other life. The myths of Idun and Kore remind us that it was the descent to death, the loss of innocence, and the estrangement from one's divine "home" that are necessary for the renewal of life. The seed appears dead, only to bring new life in the spring, and we live in the anxious hope, or even the joyful confidence, that our mortal finitude and estrangement from God and the numinous is confined to this life. The paradox is that one must die to have immortality. Idun and Kore become the bearers of spring and its power of growth only after dwelling among the dead. Similarly, Shiva, the destroyer, brings fertility and life to earth by bearing the body of the dead Sati. The New Zealand myth of Te Atarahi is a living myth because the news of immortality is community news, shared with others and providing a collective hope of new life.

It is in the myth of the hero, the mirror in which we see our own lives, that these elements are united and speak to us in terms of our individual destiny. There is little doubt of the hero's identity and participation in the cosmos. The hero claims divine fatherhood and mortal motherhood, yet is estranged from the father except for the moment of weariness and tragedy, wherein the numinous appears and the defeat is transcended. The hero must "become" a hero through facing trials from the earliest days until the quest can be realized. The hero is never alone in a story; the process of becoming a hero takes place in, with, and through others, including teachers and mentors, families, friends both true and false, and enemies. Each leaves an imprint on the process of becoming. The hero chooses to become a hero and, bound to his choices, feels their freedom and burden.

The foundation myths of states are really collective hero myths, with the heroic character shared by a people, for our identity in the cosmos has a great deal to do with our national or ethnic identity, as it is our place in the world. The elements of estrangement, becoming, and choice are writ large in the founding tales.

Thus myth is an eternal mirror in which we see our own faces. The human experience described in the myths is our experience, and they live as we live out their themes. While there is much that is tragic in these myths, there are also reasons there to find great joy and meaning in our lives. We hear voices of hope, of the power of love to transform, the good news that love is stronger than death, the sense of who we are (and how there is a thread connecting all humans in all times), the affirmation of transcendence, and the beauty of standing back from the many parts of our experience to see a wonderful whole.

The fact that myths are purposive language is at the heart of why we study them. They affirm that there is a purpose to human existence, there is a heroic process in each of us, and that each human living out that experience has value. If we are, as the myths and the traditions of our great religions tell, all God's children, we are also all heroes as we live out our quest. Our own search for love, vocation, identity, and the hope of immortality are no less a quest than that of the honored heroes. Our quest is to become all that we were meant to be, or in the words of the German philosopher Karl Jaspers, "God's will as transcendence is that I shall be my own true self, engaged in 'truthful, loving struggle.' " For as much as the hero claimed both divine and mortal parentage, we share the beautiful legacy of humanity written in the myths.

Bibliography

Akiyama, Aisaburo. *Shinto and Its Architecture*. Kyoto: Japan Welcome Society, 1936.

Arendt, Hannah. *The Life of the Mind*. 1971. Reprint, New York: Harcourt, Brace, Jovanovich, 1978.

Austin, Norman. *Meaning and Being in Myth*. University Park, Penn.: Pennsylvania State University Press, 1990.

Bachofen, J. J. *Myth, Religion, and Mother Right*. Translated by Ralph Manheim. 1973. Reprint, Princeton, N.J.: Princeton University Press, 1992.

Barbour, Ian. *Myths, Models and Paradigms*. New York: Harper and Row, 1974.

Benson, Elizabeth P. *The Maya World*. New York: Thomas Y. Crowell Co., 1967.

Berlitz, Charles. *Native Tongues*. New York: Grosset and Dunlap, 1982.

Bettelheim, Bruno. *The Uses of Enchantment*. New York: Vintage Books, 1977.

Bierlein, J. F. *The Book of Ages*. New York: Ballantine Books, 1992.

———. *Parallel Myths*. New York: Ballantine Books, 1994.

Bloom, Harold, ed. *Modern Critical Interpretations: Virgil's Aeneid*. New York: Chelsea House Publishers, 1987.

Brill, A. A., ed. *The Basic Writings of Sigmund Freud.* 1938. Reprint, New York: Modern Library, 1966.

Brittain, Frederick, ed. *The Penguin Book of Latin Verse.* Baltimore: Penguin Books, 1962.

Bultmann, Rudolf. *New Testament and Mythology and Other Basic Writings.* Selected, edited, and translated by Schubert M. Ogden. Philadelphia: Fortress Press, 1984.

Burkert, Walter. *Creation of the Sacred: Tracks of Biology in Early Religions.* Cambridge, Mass.: Harvard University Press, 1996.

Burland, Cottie A. *The Gods of Mexico.* New York: Putnam, 1967.

Campbell, Joseph, ed. *The Pocket Jung.* Translated by R.F.C. Hull. New York: Viking Press, 1972.

Cassirer, Ernst. *Language and Myth.* Translated by Susanne K. Langer. New York: Dover Publications, 1946.

Cicero. *De Natura Deorum.* Harvard Latin Classics. Cambridge, Mass.: Harvard University Press, 1955–58.

———. *The Nature of the Gods.* Translated by Horace C. P. McGregor. Harmondsworth, Middlesex, England: Penguin, 1972.

Clements, Keith W. *Friedrich Schleiermacher: Pioneer of Modern Theology.* London: Collins, 1987.

Colum, Padraic. *A Treasury of Irish Folklore.* New York: Crown Publishers, 1954.

Diaz, Bernal. *The Conquest of New Spain.* Translated by J. M. Cohen. Baltimore: Penguin, 1963.

Doty, William G. *Mythography: The Study of Myths and Rituals.* Birmingham: University of Alabama Press, 1986.

Ehrlich, Leonard H., and Richard Wisser. *The Philosophy of Karl Jaspers.* Pittsburgh: Center for Advanced Research in Phenomenology; Lanham, Md.: University Press of America, 1988.

Eliade, Mircea. *Myth and Reality.* Translated by Willard R. Trask. New York: Harper and Row, 1963.

Fischer, Klaus P. *Nazi Germany: A New History.* New York: Continuum, 1995.

Freidel, David, Linda Schele, and Joy Parker. *Maya Crossings.* New York: William Morrow and Co., 1993.

Friederich, Werner P. *History of German Literature*. New York: Barnes and Noble, 1961.

Friedman, Maurice, ed. *The Worlds of Existentialism*. New York: Random House, 1964.

Gaddis, Vincent H. *American Indian Myths and Mysteries*. Radnor, Pa.: The Chilton Book Company, 1977.

Gantz, Jeffrey, trans. *Early Irish Myths and Sagas*. New York and Harmondsworth, Middlesex, England: Penguin, 1981.

Goethe, Johann Wolfgang von. *Faust: Eine Tragödie (Erster und Zweiter Teil)*. Munich: Deutscher Taschenbuch Verlag, 1977.

Hatab, Lawrence J. *Myth and Philosophy: A Contest of Truths*. La Salle, Ill.: Open Court, 1990.

Hearn, Lafcadio. *Japan's Religions: Shinto and Buddhism*. New Hyde Park, N.Y.: University Books, 1966.

———. *The Religions of Japan*. Rutland, Vt.: Charles Tuttle, 1953.

Herm, Gerhard. *The Celts*. New York: St. Martin's Press, 1977.

Hesiod. *Theogony and the Works and the Days*. Translated by Richmond Lattimore. Ann Arbor: University of Michigan Press, 1959.

Hinks, Roger. *Myth and Allegory in Ancient Art*. 1939. Reprint, London: The Warburg Institute, 1955.

Hirsch, E. D., Jr. *Cultural Literacy*. Boston: Houghton Mifflin, 1987.

Jaspers, Karl. *Basic Philosophical Writings*. Translated by Edith Ehrlich, Leonard H. Ehrlich, and George B. Pepper. Atlantic Highlands, N.J.: Humanities Press, 1994.

———. *Tragedy Is Not Enough*. Translated by Harald A. T. Reiche, Harry T. Moore, and Karl Deutsch. Hamden, Conn.: Archon Books, 1969.

———. *Was Ist Philosophie? Ein Lesebuch*. München; Zürich: Piper, 1976.

Johnson, Roger A. *Rudolf Bultmann: Interpreting Faith for the Modern Era*. London: Collins, 1987.

Jüngel, Eberhard. *Barth-Studien*. Zürich and Cologne: Benziger Verlag, 1982.

Lowrie, Donald A., trans. *Christian Existentialism: A Berdyaev Anthology.* New York: Harper, 1965.

Lowrie, Walter. *Art in the Early Church.* New York: Pantheon Books, 1947.

Malraux, André. *The Voices of Silence.* Translated by Stuart Gilbert. 1953. Reprint, Princeton, N.J.: Princeton University Press, 1978.

Marcel, Gabriel. *The Philosophy of Existentialism.* Translated by Manya Harari. 1956. Reprint, New York: Citadel Press, 1988.

Maritain, Jacques. *Art and Scholasticism and the Frontiers of Poetry.* Translated by Joseph W. Evans. New York: Charles Scribner's Sons, 1962.

Mason, J.W.T. *The Spirit of Shinto Mythology.* Tokyo: Fuzambo Co., 1939.

Mathews, Thomas F. *The Clash of Gods.* Princeton, N.J.: Princeton University Press, 1993.

Neumann, Erich. *Art and the Creative Unconscious.* Translated by Ralph Manheim. Princeton, N.J.: Princeton University Press, 1971.

Nietzsche, Friedrich. *Also Sprach Zarathustra.* Munich: Wilhelm Goldmann Verlag, n.d.

Ono, Motonori. *Shinto: The Kami Way.* Tokyo and Rutland, Vt.: Bridgeway Press, 1962.

Ortega y Gasset, José. *El Tema de Nuestro Tiempo.* Buenos Aires: México Espasa-Calpe, 1939.

Otto, Walter F. *Die Gestalt und das Sein.* Darmstadt: Wissenschaftliche Buchgesellschaft, 1959.

Ovid. *Metamorphoses.* Translated by Mary M. Innes. London and New York: Penguin Books, 1955.

Packard, Jerrold M. *Sons of Heaven: A Portrait of the Japanese Monarchy.* New York: Charles Scribner's Sons, 1987.

Peterson, Richard F. *William Butler Yeats.* Twayne's English Authors Series. Boston: Twayne Publishers, 1982.

Rank, Otto. *The Myth of the Birth of the Hero and Other Writings.* Edited by Philip Freund. New York: Vintage Books, 1959.

Ricoeur, Paul. *Fallible Man.* Chicago: Henry Regnery, 1965.

————. *The Symbolism of Evil*. Boston: Beacon Press, 1967.

Rienecker, Fritz. *Lexikon zur Bibel*. 1960. Reprint, Wuppertal: R. Brockhaus Verlag, 1992.

Robertson, John G. *A History of German Literature*. New York: G. P. Putnam's Sons, 1902.

Shirer, William. *The Rise and Fall of the Third Reich*. New York: Simon and Schuster, 1960.

Skene, Reg. *The Cuchulain Plays of W. B. Yeats: A Study*. New York: Columbia University Press, 1974.

Smith, Homer W. *Man and His Gods*. Boston: Little, Brown and Co., 1952.

Toland, John. *The Rising Sun: The Decline and Fall of the Japanese Empire*. New York: Random House, 1970.

Uhland, Ludwig. *Tannhaeuser*. Munich: Deutscher Taschenbuch Verlag, 1974.

Unamuno, Miguel de. *El Porvenir de España y los Españoles*. Madrid: Colleccion Austral/Espasa-Calpe S.A., 1978.

Varley, H. Paul. *Japanese Culture: A Short History*. New York: Praeger, 1973.

Virgil. *The Aeneid*. Translated by Allen Mandelbaum. Berkeley: University of California Press, 1971.

Wach, Joachim. *The Comparative Study of Religions*. New York: Columbia University Press, 1958.

Yeats, W. B. *The Poems of W. B. Yeats*. Edited by Richard Finneran. New York: Macmillan and Company, 1983.

Index

ethical dilemma in, 153–54
of hero, 120, 122, 152
risks in, 5–6, 120
Clymene, mother of Phaëthon, 28
Community, challenged, 13, 36–40
Conchobar, King, 122, 139, 140, 141, 152
Connla, 143–44, 152, 216
Conscience, 82
Constellations, 30, 32, 160
Corinth, 124, 126
Cornwall, 204
Cortéz, Hernando, 166
Cosmos, human place in, 3
death/rebirth cycle, 91, 97
domain of nature, 90, 91
and heroes, 120
and myths, 6–7, 11, 14, 90
symbolized, 166
See also Identity
Creation myths
Algonquin, 53, 105
Chinese, 176
See also Kojiki
Crete, 123–24, 127
Cronus, god, 54
Cuchulain, hero, 138–52
betrayal of, 122–23
birth/childhood, 120–22, 139
cultural values, 158
and Emer, 79–82, 141–42, 143
and Ferdia, 142–43, 149–52
Gai-bolga, 142, 143, 148, 151
geissa, 143–44, 146, 152, 153–54, 216
transcendence, 123, 148–49, 217
trials of, 144–52
youth, 139–44, 152, 209
Cupid, 58–61, 64, 71

Daedalus, builder, 127, 128
the Dagda, king of gods, 74
Daksha prajapati, 98–101, 102, 103
Dalan, druid, 77
Damayanti, 43–52
and five Nalas, 45–46, 79
marriage to mortal, 74
swayamvara, 43–46, 50–52
transforming love, 52–54, 78, 219
Dardanus, ancestor, 196
De Lamartine, Alphonse, 5
De Landa, Bishop, 159
Death
conquered by love, 137
of growing season, 96–97, 110
inevitability of, 4, 34, 89, 97

linked to estrangement, 21
as passageway, 92
transcendence in grief, 103
See also Finitude
Death/rebirth cycle, 91
Kore, myth of, 105, 210–20
life after death, 10, 118, 138
and place in cosmos, 91, 97
Sati, myth of, 102–3, 105, 220
and seasons, 92–97, 105
symbolic, 115
See also Resurrection
Deimos, son of Aphrodite, 55, 71
Delphi, oracle of, 59
Demeter, goddess, 28, 92–96, 98, 102, 191
Demons, 46, 49, 53, 80
Dialogue, I-thou, 42
Diana, goddess, 195, 203
See also Artemis
Diaz, Bernal, 165
Dido, Queen, 196–97, 199
The Dioscuri, 131–32, 134–35
Dis. See Pluto
Discord, spirit, 198, 199
Disease, underworld spirit, 198
Druids, 77, 139, 140, 145
Dushyanta, King, 181–85

Eagles, 63, 106–7, 108, 168, 169
Early Irish Myths and Sagas (Gantz), 82
Earth
as deity, Korea, 179
jeopardized. See Natural disasters
Mother Earth, 32, 94, 95
Earth Element Day, 177
Eckhardt, 66, 68
Eclipse, solar, 114
Egypt
death of firstborn, 19
Jewish exodus, 11, 19
Two Brothers tale, 14, 137
Eleusinian Mysteries, 95–97
Elizabeth, 66–69, 70, 71–72
Emer, wife of Cuchulain, as warrior, 79, 81–82
Eochy, High King, 75–78
Eris, goddess of discord, 57, 71
Eros. See Cupid
Estrangement, from numinous
of hero, 120, 137
human condition of, 3, 11
reconciliation of, 4
and sacrifices, 13, 21

About the Author

The author of *Parallel Myths* and *The Book of Ages*, J. F. BIERLEIN is presently working on his next book, a study of world mythology and beliefs regarding the afterlife. He teaches in the Washington Semester and World Capitals Program at American University in Washington, and also works for a social sciences consulting firm. He is presently lecturing on mythology at the Smithsonian Institution in Washington.

Multilingual, he is deeply interested in theology, existentialism, art, opera, and the study of classical Greek, Sanskrit, and Hebrew, as well as other languages.

Professor Bierlein and his wife, Heather Diehl, live in northern Virginia.

And don't miss Jean Houston's classic book

THE HERO AND THE GODDESS
The Odyssey as Mystery and Initiation

"Houston has broken through to a new understanding of the sense and uses of the disciplines of inward-turned contemplation. . . . She gets people to awaken themselves to unknown powers that transform their lives."
—JOSEPH CAMPBELL

The Hero and the Goddess explores the transformational power of one of the world's greatest stories—*The Odyssey.* This classic tale of adventures and exploits is the supreme metaphor in the Western mind for spiritual initiation. Jean Houston interprets each episode from the epic—including Odysseus's confrontation with the Cyclops, his temptation by the Sirens, his descent into the Underworld, and his ultimate reunion with the subtle and brilliant Penelope—and explores with us the universal themes of wounding and betrayal, suffering and loss, terrifying triumph and the search for the Divine Beloved. Through detailed exercises and dramatic enactments that can be done in groups or alone, *The Hero and the Goddess* guides us to our journey's end—renewed, reborn, and rededicated to the possibilities our lives offer.

Available in bookstores everywhere.
Published by Ballantine Wellspring
The Ballantine Publishing Group
www.randomhouse.com/BB